FOSSILS Keith Thomson
FOUCAULT Gary Gutting
FREE SPEECH ...
FREE WILL Th...
FRENCH LITER...
THE FRENCH ...
    William Doyle
FREUD Anthony Storr
FUNDAMENTALISM Malise Ruthven
GALAXIES John Gribbin
GALILEO Stillman Drake
GAME THEORY Ken Binmore
GANDHI Bhikhu Parekh
GEOGRAPHY John Matthews and
    David Herbert
GEOPOLITICS Klaus Dodds
GERMAN LITERATURE Nicholas Boyle
GERMAN PHILOSOPHY Andrew Bowie
GLOBAL CATASTROPHES Bill McGuire
GLOBAL WARMING Mark Maslin
GLOBALIZATION Manfred Steger
THE GREAT DEPRESSION AND THE
    NEW DEAL Eric Rauchway
HABERMAS James Gordon Finlayson
HEGEL Peter Singer
HEIDEGGER Michael Inwood
HIEROGLYPHS Penelope Wilson
HINDUISM Kim Knott
HISTORY John H. Arnold
THE HISTORY OF ASTRONOMY
    Michael Hoskin
THE HISTORY OF LIFE Michael Benton
THE HISTORY OF MEDICINE
    William Bynum
THE HISTORY OF TIME
    Leofranc Holford-Strevens
HIV/AIDS Alan Whiteside
HOBBES RICHARD TUCKHUMAN
    EVOLUTION Bernard Wood
HUMANISM Stephen Law
HUMAN RIGHTS Andrew Clapham
HUME A. J. Ayer
IDEOLOGY Michael Freeden
INDIAN PHILOSOPHY Sue Hamilton
INFORMATION Luciano Floridi
INNOVATION Mark Dodgson and
    David Gann
INTELLIGENCE Ian J. Deary
INTERNATIONAL MIGRATION
    Khalid Koser
INTERNATIONAL RELATIONS
    Paul Wilkinson

...hven
Y Adam Silverstein
Hargreaves
Solomon
...ony Stevens
KABBALAH Joseph Dan
KAFKA Ritchie Robertson
KANT Roger Scruton
KEYNES Robert Skidelsky
KIERKEGAARD Patrick Gardiner
THE KORAN Michael Cook
LANDSCAPES AND GEOMORPHOLOGY
    Andrew Goudie and Heather Viles
LATE ANTIQUITY Gillian Clark
LAW Raymond Wacks
THE LAWS OF THERMODYNAMICS
    Peter Atkins
LEADERSHIP Keith Grint
LINCOLN Allen C. Guelzo
LINGUISTICS Peter Matthews
LITERARY THEORY Jonathan Culler
LOCKE John Dunn
LOGIC Graham Priest
MACHIAVELLI Quentin Skinner
THE MARQUIS DE SADE John Phillips
MARX Peter Singer
MARTIN LUTHER Scott H. Hendrix
MATHEMATICS Timothy Gowers
THE MEANING OF LIFE Terry Eagleton
MEDICAL ETHICS Tony Hope
MEDIEVAL BRITAIN John Gillingham and
    Ralph A. Griffiths
MEMORY JONATHAN K. Foster
MICHAEL FARADAY Frank A. J. L. James
MODERN ART David Cottington
MODERN CHINA Rana Mitter
MODERN IRELAND Senia Pašeta
MODERN JAPAN Christopher Goto-Jones
MODERNISM Christopher Butler
MOLECULES Philip Ball
MORMONISM Richard Lyman Bushman
MUHAMMAD Jonathan A. Brown
MUSIC Nicholas Cook
MYTH Robert A. Segal
NATIONALISM Steven Grosby
NELSON MANDELA Elleke Boehmer
NEOLIBERALISM Manfred Steger and
    Ravi Roy
THE NEW TESTAMENT
    Luke Timothy Johnson
THE NEW TESTAMENT AS LITERATURE
    Kyle Keefer

NEWTON Robert Iliffe
NIETZSCHE Michael Tanner
NINETEENTH-CENTURY BRITAIN
 Christopher Harvie and H.C.G. Matthew
THE NORMAN CONQUEST
 George Garnett
NORTH AMERICAN INDIANS
 Theda Perdue and Michael D. Green
NORTHERN IRELAND Marc Mulholland
NOTHING Frank Close
NUCLEAR WEAPONS Joseph M. Siracusa
THE OLD TESTAMENT
 Michael D. Coogan
PARTICLE PHYSICS Frank Close
PAUL E.P. Sanders
PENTECOSTALISM William K. Kay
PHILOSOPHY Edward Craig
PHILOSOPHY OF LAW Raymond Wacks
PHILOSOPHY OF SCIENCE Samir Okasha
PHOTOGRAPHY Steve Edwards
PLANETS David A. Rothery
PLATO Julia Annas
POLITICAL PHILOSOPHY David Miller
POLITICS Kenneth Minogue
POSTCOLONIALISM Robert Young
POSTMODERNISM Christopher Butler
POSTSTRUCTURALISM Catherine Belsey
PREHISTORY Chris Gosden
PRESOCRATIC PHILOSOPHY
 Catherine Osborne
PRIVACY Raymond Wacks
PROGRESSIVISM Walter Nugent
PSYCHIATRY Tom Burns
PSYCHOLOGY Gillian Butler and
 Freda McManus
PURITANISM Francis J. Bremer
THE QUAKERS Pink Dandelion
QUANTUM THEORY John Polkinghorne
RACISM Ali Rattansi
THE REAGAN REVOLUTION Gil Troy
THE REFORMATION Peter Marshall
RELATIVITY Russell Stannard
RELIGION IN AMERICA Timothy Beal
THE RENAISSANCE Jerry Brotton
RENAISSANCE ART Geraldine A. Johnson
RISK Baruch Fischhoff and John Kadvany

ROMAN BRITAIN Peter Salway
THE ROMAN EMPIRE Christopher Kelly
ROMANTICISM Michael Ferber
ROUSSEAU Robert Wokler
RUSSELL A.C. Grayling
RUSSIAN LITERATURE Catriona Kelly
THE RUSSIAN REVOLUTION S.A. Smith
SCHIZOPHRENIA Chris Frith and
 Eve Johnstone
SCHOPENHAUER Christopher Janaway
SCIENCE AND RELIGION Thomas Dixon
SCOTLAND Rab Houston
SEXUALITY Véronique Mottier
SHAKESPEARE Germaine Greer
SOCIAL AND CULTURAL
 ANTHROPOLOGY John Monaghan
 and Peter Just
SOCIALISM Michael Newman
SOCIOLOGY Steve Bruce
SOCRATES C.C.W. Taylor
THE SOVIET UNION Stephen Lovell
THE SPANISH CIVIL WAR Helen Graham
SPANISH LITERATURE Jo Labanyi
SPINOZA Roger Scruton
STATISTICS David J. Hand
STUART BRITAIN John Morrill
SUPERCONDUCTIVITY Stephen Blundell
TERRORISM Charles Townshend
THEOLOGY David F. Ford
THOMAS AQUINAS Fergus Kerr
TOCQUEVILLE Harvey C. Mansfield
TRAGEDY Adrian Poole
THE TUDORS John Guy
TWENTIETH-CENTURY BRITAIN
 Kenneth O. Morgan
THE UNITED NATIONS
 Jussi M. Hanhimäki
THE U.S. CONGRESS Donald A. Ritchie
UTOPIANISM Lyman Tower Sargent
THE VIKINGS Julian Richards
WITCHCRAFT Malcolm Gaskill
WITTGENSTEIN A.C. Grayling
WORLD MUSIC Philip Bohlman
THE WORLD TRADE ORGANIZATION
 Amrita Narlikar
WRITING AND SCRIPT Andrew Robinson

For more information visit our web site:
www.oup.co.uk/general/vsi/

Peter Singer

MARX

A Very Short Introduction

OXFORD
UNIVERSITY PRESS

OXFORD
UNIVERSITY PRESS

Great Clarendon Street, Oxford OX2 6DP

Oxford University Press is a department of the University of Oxford.
It furthers the University's objective of excellence in research, scholarship,
and education by publishing worldwide in

Oxford New York

Auckland Bangkok Buenos Aires Cape Town Chennai
Dar es Salaam Delhi Hong Kong Istanbul Karachi Kolkata
Kuala Lumpur Madrid Melbourne Mexico City Mumbai Nairobi
São Paulo Shanghai Taipei Tokyo Toronto

Oxford is a registered trade mark of Oxford University Press
in the UK and in certain other countries

Published in the United States
by Oxford University Press Inc., New York

First published 1980 as an Oxford University Press paperback
Reissued 1996
First published as a Very Short Introduction 2000

British Library Cataloguing in Publication Data

Data available

Library of Congress Cataloging in Publication Data

Data available

ISBN 978-0-19-285405-6

18 19

Typeset by RefineCatch Ltd, Bungay, Suffolk
Printed in Great Britain by
Ashford Colour Press Ltd, Gosport, Hants.

Contents

Preface ix

Abbreviations xi

List of Illustrations xiii

1 A Life and its Impact 1

2 The Young Hegelian 16

3 From God to Money 23

4 Enter the Proletariat 28

5 The First Marxism 32

6 Alienation as a Theory of History 39

7 The Goal of History 47

8 Economics 59

9 Communism 78

10 An Assessment 86

Note on Sources 101

Further Reading 103

Index 106

Preface

There are many books on Marx, but a good brief introduction to his thought is still hard to find. Marx wrote at such enormous length, on so many different subjects, that it is not easy to see his ideas as a whole. I believe that there is a central idea, a vision of the world, which unifies all of Marx's thought and explains what would otherwise be puzzling features of it. In this book I try to say, in terms comprehensible to those with little or no previous knowledge of Marx's writings, what this central vision is. If I have succeeded, I need no further excuse for having added yet another book to the already abundant literature on Marx and Marxism.

For biographical details of Marx's life, I am especially indebted to David McLellan's fine work, *Karl Marx: His Life and Thought* (Macmillan, London, 1973). My view of Marx's conception of history was affected by G.A. Cohen's *Karl Marx's Theory of History: A Defence* (Oxford University Press, Oxford, 1979), although I do not accept all the conclusions of that challenging study. Gerald Cohen sent me detailed comments on the draft of this book, enabling me to correct several errors. Robert Heilbroner, Renata Singer, and Marilyn Weltz also made helpful comments on the draft, for which I am grateful.

In the interest of clear prose I have occasionally made minor amendments to the translations of Marx's works from which I have quoted.

Finally, were it not for an invitation to take part in this series from Keith Thomas, the general editor of the series, and Henry Hardy, of Oxford University Press, I would never have attempted to write this book; and were it not for a period of leave granted me by Monash University, I would never have written it.

Peter Singer
Washington, DC, June 1979

Abbreviations

References in the text to Marx's writings are generally given by an abbreviation of the title, followed by a page reference. Unless otherwise indicated below, these page references are to David McLellan (ed.), *Karl Marx: Selected Writings* (Oxford University Press, Oxford, 1977).

B	'On Bakunin's *Statism and Anarchy*'
C I	*Capital*, Volume I (Foreign Languages Publishing House, Moscow, 1961)
C III	*Capital*, Volume III
CM	*Communist Manifesto*
D	Doctoral thesis
EB	*The Eighteenth Brumaire of Louis Bonaparte*
EPM	*Economic and Philosophical Manuscripts of 1844*
G	*Grundrisse* (translated M. Nicolaus, Penguin, Harmondsworth, 1973)
GI	*The German Ideology*
GP	'Critique of the Gotha Program'
I	'Towards a Critique of Hegel's *Philosophy of Right*: Introduction'
J	'On the Jewish Question'
M	'On James Mill' (notebook)
MC	Letters and miscellaneous writings cited in David McLellan, *Karl Marx: His Life and Thought* (Macmillan, London, 1973)
P	Preface to *A Contribution to the Critique of Political Economy*

PP	*The Poverty of Philosophy*
R	Correspondence with Ruge of 1843
T	'Theses on Feuerbach'
WLC	*Wage Labour and Capital*
WPP	'Wages, Price and Profit' (in K. Marx, F. Engels, *Selected Works*, Foreign Languages Publishing House, Moscow, 1951)

List of Illustrations

1   Karl Marx (1818–83)   2

2   Lithograph showing the
    young Marx (1836) at a
    drinking club of Trier
    students at the University
    of Bonn   4
    Courtesy of the International
    Institute of Social History,
    Amsterdam

3   The exterior of 41 Maitland
    Park Road, Haverstock Hill,
    London, where Marx spent
    the last fifteen years of his
    life   13
    Courtesy of Hulton Getty

4   Marx with his eldest
    daughter, Jenny, in 1870   14
    Courtesy of Hulton Getty

5   G. W. F. Hegel
    (1770–1831)   19

6   Marx in 1836, aged 18.
    Detail from the lithograph
    on p. 4   26
    Courtesy of the International
    Institute of Social History,
    Amsterdam

7   Ludwig Feuerbach
    (1804–72)   42
    Courtesy of the Mary Evans Picture
    Library

8   Friedrich Engels
    (1820–95)   45

9   English factories in the
    mid-nineteenth century:
    men and women at work in
    the Patent Renewable
    Stocking Factory at
    Tewkesbury in 1860   53
    Courtesy of the Mary Evans Picture
    Library

10   David Ricardo
      (1772– 1823)   65
      Courtesy of Hulton Getty

11   The round reading room of
      the old British Library, opened
      in 1842, where Marx worked
      on *Das Kapital*   69
      Courtesy of Hulton Getty

12   Cover of the first German
      edition of *Das Kapital*,
      vol. 1   75
      Courtesy of AKG London

13   Marx's grave at Highgate
      Cemetery in London   87
      Courtesy of Hulton Getty

14   Joseph Stalin
      (1879–1953)   96
      Courtesy of Hulton Getty

15   Military tanks passing a
      mural of key communist
      figures in a 1974 parade in
      Havana, Cuba, marking the
      anniversary of the
      Revolution   98
      Courtesy of Miroslav Zaji/Corbis

The publisher and the author apologize for any errors or omissions in the above list. If contacted they will be pleased to rectify these at the earliest opportunity.

Chapter 1
A Life and its Impact

Marx's impact can only be compared with that of religious figures like Jesus or Muhammad. For much of the second half of the twentieth century, nearly four of of every ten people on earth lived under governments that considered themselves Marxist and claimed – however implausibly – to use Marxist principles to decide how the nation should be run. In these countries Marx was a kind of secular Jesus; his writings were the ultimate source of truth and authority; his image was everywhere reverently displayed. The lives of hundreds of millions of people have been deeply affected by Marx's legacy.

Nor has Marx's influence been limited to communist societies. Conservative governments have ushered in social reforms to cut the ground from under revolutionary Marxist opposition movements. Conservatives have also reacted in less benign ways: Mussolini and Hitler were helped to power by conservatives who saw their rabid nationalism as the answer to the Marxist threat. And even when there was no threat of an internal revolution, the existence of a foreign Marxist enemy served to justify governments in increasing arms spending and restricting individual rights in the name of national security.

1. Karl Marx (1818–83)

On the level of thought rather than practical politics, Marx's contribution is equally evident. Can anyone now think about society without reference to Marx's insights into the links between economic and intellectual life? Marx's ideas brought about modern sociology, transformed the study of history, and profoundly affected philosophy, literature, and the arts. In this sense of the term – admittedly a very loose sense – we are all Marxists now.

What were the ideas that had such far-reaching effects? That is the subject of this book. But first, a little about the man who had these ideas.

Karl Marx was born in Trier, in the German Rhineland, in 1818. His parents, Heinrich and Henrietta, were of Jewish origin but became nominally Protestant in order to make life easier for Heinrich to practise law. The family was comfortably off without being really wealthy; they held liberal, but not radical, views on religion and politics.

Marx's intellectual career began badly when, at the age of seventeen, he went to study law at the University of Bonn. Within a year he had been imprisoned for drunkenness and slightly wounded in a duel. He also wrote love poems to his childhood sweetheart, Jenny von Westphalen. His father had soon had enough of this 'wild rampaging' as he called it, and decided that Karl should transfer to the more serious University of Berlin.

In Berlin Marx's interests became more intellectual, and his studies turned from law to philosophy. This did not impress his father: 'degeneration in a learned dressing-gown with uncombed hair has replaced degeneration with a beer glass' he wrote in a reproving letter (MC 33). It was, however, the death rather than the reproaches of his father that forced Marx to think seriously about a career – for without his father's income the family could not afford to support him

3

2. Lithograph showing the young Marx (1836) at a drinking club of Trier students at the University of Bonn

indefinitely. Marx therefore began work on a doctoral thesis with a view to getting a university lectureship. The thesis itself was on a remote and scholarly topic – some contrasts in the philosophies of Democritus and Epicurus – but Marx saw a parallel between these ancient disputes and the debate about the interpretation of the philosophy of Hegel which was at that time the meeting ground of divergent political views in German thought.

The thesis was submitted and accepted in 1841, but no university lectureship was offered. Instead Marx became interested in journalism. He wrote on social, political, and philosophical issues for a newly founded liberal newspaper, the *Rhenish Gazette* (*Rheinische Zeitung*). His articles were appreciated and his contacts with the newspaper increased to such an extent that when the editor resigned late in 1842, Marx was the obvious replacement.

Through no fault of his own, Marx's editorship was brief. As interest in the newspaper increased, so did the attentions of the Prussian government censor. A series of articles by Marx on the poverty of wine-growers in the Moselle valley may have been considered especially inflammatory; in any case, the government decided to suppress the paper.

Marx was not sorry that the authorities had, as he put it in a letter to a friend, 'given me back my liberty' (MC 66). Freed from editorial duties, he began work on a critical study of Hegel's political philosophy. He also had a more pressing concern: to marry Jenny, to whom he had now been engaged for seven years. And he wanted to leave Germany, where he could not express himself freely. The problem was that he needed money to get married, and now he was again unemployed. But his reputation as a promising young writer stood him in good stead; he was invited to become co-editor of a new publication, the *German–French Annals* (*Deutsch–Französische Jahrbücher*). This provided him with enough income to marry and also settled the question of where to go – for, as its name implies, the new publication was supposed to draw French as well as German writers and readers.

Karl and Jenny Marx arrived in Paris in the autumn of 1843 and soon began mixing with the radicals and socialists who congregated in this centre of progressive thought. Marx wrote two articles for the *Annals*. The publication was, however, even more short-lived than the newspaper had been. The first issue failed to attract any French contributors and so was scarcely noticed in Paris; while copies sent to Prussia were confiscated by the authorities. The financial backers of the venture withdrew. Meanwhile, in view of the communist and revolutionary ideas expressed in the confiscated first issue, the Prussian government issued a warrant for the arrest of the editors. Now Marx could not return to Germany; he was a political refugee. Luckily he received a sizeable amount of money from the former shareholders of the *Rhenish Gazette*, so he had no need of a job.

Throughout 1844 Marx worked at articulating his philosophical position. This was philosophy in a very broad sense, including politics, economics, and a conception of the historical processes at work in the world. By now Marx was prepared to call himself a communist – which was nothing very unusual in those days in Paris, for socialists and communists of all sorts could be found there then.

In the same year the friendship between Marx and Engels began. Friedrich Engels was the son of a German industrialist who also owned a cotton factory in Manchester; but Engels had become, through contacts with the same German intellectual circles that Marx moved in, a revolutionary socialist. He contributed an article to the *Annals* which deeply affected Marx's own thinking about economics. So it was not surprising that when Engels visited Paris he and Marx should meet. Very soon they began to collaborate on a pamphlet – or rather Engels thought it was going to be a pamphlet. He left his contribution, about fifteen pages long, with Marx when he departed from Paris. The 'pamphlet' appeared under the title *The Holy Family* in 1845. Almost 300 pages long, it was Marx's first published book.

Meanwhile the Prussian government was putting pressure on the French to do something about the German communists living in Paris. An expulsion order was issued and the Marx family, which now included their first child, named Jenny like her mother, moved to Brussels.

To obtain permission to stay in Brussels, Marx had to promise not to take part in politics. He soon breached this undertaking by organizing a Communist Correspondence Committee which was intended to keep communists in different countries in touch with each other. Nevertheless Marx was able to stay in Brussels for three years. He signed a contract with a publisher to produce a book consisting of a critical analysis of economics and politics. The contract called for the book to be ready by the summer of 1845. It was the first of many deadlines missed by the book that was to become *Capital*. The publisher had, no doubt to his lasting regret, undertaken to pay royalties in advance of receiving the manuscript. (The contract was eventually cancelled, and the unfortunate man was still trying to get his money back in 1871.) Engels also now began to help Marx financially, so the family had enough to live on.

Marx and Engels saw a good deal of each other. Engels came to Brussels, and then the two of them travelled to England for six weeks to study economics in Manchester, the heart of the new industrial age. (Meanwhile Jenny was bearing Marx their second daughter, Laura.) On his return Marx decided to postpone his book on economics. Before setting forth his own positive theory, he wanted to demolish alternative ideas then fashionable in German philosophical and socialist circles. The outcome was *The German Ideology*, a long and often turgid volume which was turned down by at least seven publishers and finally abandoned, as Marx later wrote, 'to the gnawing criticism of the mice'.

In addition to writing *The German Ideology*, Marx spent a good deal of these years attacking those who might have been his allies. He wrote another polemical work attacking the leading French socialist, Proudhon. Though theoretically opposed to what he called 'a superstitious attitude to authority' (MC 172), Marx was so convinced of the importance of his own ideas that he could not tolerate opinions different from his own. This led to frequent rows in the Communist Correspondence Committee and in the Communist League which followed it.

Marx had an opportunity to make his own ideas the basis of communist activities when he went to London, to attend a Congress of the newly formed Communist League in December 1847. In lengthy debates he defended his view of how communism would come about; and in the end he and Engels were commissioned with the task of putting down the doctrines of the League in simple language. The result was *The Communist Manifesto*, published in February 1848, which was to become the classic outline of Marx's theory.

The *Manifesto* was not, however, an immediate success. Before it could be published the situation in Europe had been transformed by the French revolution of 1848, which triggered off revolutionary movements all over Europe. The new French government revoked Marx's expulsion order, just as the nervous Belgian government gave him twenty-four hours to get out of the country. The Marxes went first to Paris and then, following news of revolution in Berlin, returned to Germany. In Cologne Marx raised money to start a radical newspaper, the *New Rhenish Gazette* (*Neue Rheinische Zeitung*). The paper supported the broad democratic movements that had made the revolution. It flourished for a time, but as the revolution fizzled out the Prussian monarchy reasserted itself and Marx was compelled to set out on his travels again. He tried Paris, only to be expelled once more; so on 24 August 1849 he sailed for England to wait until a more thoroughgoing revolution would allow him to return to Germany.

Marx lived in London for the rest of his life. The family was at first quite poor. They lived in two rooms in Soho. Jenny was pregnant with their fourth child (a son, Edgar, had been born in Brussels). Nevertheless Marx was active politically with the Communist League. He wrote on the revolution in France and its aftermath, and attempted to organize support for members of the Cologne Committee of the League, who had been put on trial by the Prussian authorities. When the Cologne group were convicted, notwithstanding Marx's clear demonstration that the police evidence was forged, Marx decided that the League's existence was 'no longer opportune' and the League dissolved itself.

For a while Marx lived an isolated existence, unconnected with any organized political group. He spent his time reading omnivorously and engaging in doctrinal squabbles with other left-wing German refugees. His correspondence is full of complaints of being able to afford nothing but bread and potatoes and little enough of those. He even applied for a job as a railway clerk, but was turned down because his handwriting was illegible. He was a regular client of the pawnshops. Yet Marx's friends, especially Engels, were generous in their gifts, and it may be that Marx's poverty was due to poor management rather than insufficient income. Jenny's maid, Helene Demuth, still lived with the family, as she was to do until Marx's death. (She was also the mother of Marx's illegitimate son, Frederick, who was born in 1851; to avoid scandal, the boy was raised by foster parents.)

These were years of personal tragedy for the family: their fourth child had died in infancy; Jenny became pregnant again, and this child died within a year. The worst blow was the death of their son Edgar, apparently of consumption, at the age of eight.

From 1852 Marx received a steadier income. The editor of the *New York Tribune*, whom he had met in Cologne, asked him to write for the newspaper. Marx agreed, and over the next ten years the *Tribune* published an article by Marx almost every week (although some were secretly written by Engels). In 1856 the financial situation improved still further when Jenny received two inheritances. Now the family could move from the cramped Soho rooms to an eight-room house near Hampstead Heath, the scene of regular Sunday picnics for all the family. In this year Marx's third daughter, Eleanor – nicknamed Tussy – was born. Although Jenny was to become pregnant one more time, the child was stillborn. From this time on, therefore, the family consisted of three children: Jenny, Laura, and Eleanor. Marx was a warm and loving father to them.

All this time Marx was expecting a revolution to break out in the near future. His most productive period, in 1857–8, resulted from his mistaking an economic depression for the onset of the final crisis of capitalism. Worried that his ideas would be overtaken by events, Marx began, as he wrote to Engels, 'working madly through the nights' in order to have the outlines of his work clear 'before the deluge' (MC 290). In six months he wrote more than 800 pages of a draft of *Capital* – indeed the draft covers much more ground than *Capital* as it finally appeared. In 1859 Marx published a small portion of his work on economics under the title *Critique of Political Economy*. The book did not contain much of Marx's original ideas (except for a now famous summary of his intellectual development in the preface) and its appearance was greeted with silence.

Instead of getting the remaining, more original sections of his manuscript ready for publication, Marx was distracted by a characteristic feud with a left-wing politician and editor, Karl Vogt. Marx claimed that Vogt was in the pay of the French government. Lawsuits resulted, Vogt called Marx a forger and blackmailer, and Marx replied with a 200-page book of satirical anti-Vogt polemic. Years later, Marx was shown to have been right; but the affair cost him a good deal of money and for eighteen months prevented him writing anything of lasting value.

There was also a more serious reason for Marx's tardiness in completing his work on economics. The International Workingmen's Association – later known as the First International – was founded at a public meeting in London in 1864. Marx accepted an invitation to the meeting; his election to the General Council ended his isolation from political activities. Marx's forceful intellect and strength of personality soon made him a dominant figure in the association. He wrote its inaugural address and drew up its statutes. He had, of course, considerable differences with the trade unionists who formed the basis of the English section of the International, but he showed rare diplomacy in accommodating these differences while trying constantly to draw the working-class members of the association closer to his own long-term perspective.

In 1867 Marx finally completed the first volume of *Capital*. Again, the initial reaction was disappointing. Marx's friends were enthusiastic and did what they could to get the book reviewed. Engels alone wrote seven different – but always favourable – reviews for seven German newspapers. But wider recognition came slowly. In fact Marx became a well-known figure not because of *Capital*, but through the publication, in 1871, of *The Civil War in France*. Marx wrote this as an address to the International on the Paris Commune, the workers' uprising which, after the defeat of France at the hands of Prussia, took over and ruled the city of Paris for two months. The International had had virtually nothing to do with this, but it was linked with the Commune in the popular mind. Marx's address reinforced these early suspicions of an international communist conspiracy, and Marx himself immediately gained a notoriety which, as he wrote to a friend, 'really does me good after the tedious twenty-year idyll in my den' (MC 402).

The ruthless suppression of the Commune weakened the International. Disagreements that had simmered beneath the surface now rose to the top. At the Congress of 1872, Marx found that he had lost control. A motion restricting the powers of the General Council was carried over his strong opposition. Rather than see the organization fall into the hands of his enemies, Marx proposed that the General Council should henceforth be based in New York. The motion was passed by a narrow margin. It meant, as Marx must have known it would, the end of the First International; for with communications as they then were, it was utterly impractical to run the largely European organization from across the Atlantic.

By this time Marx was fifty-four years old and in poor health. The remaining ten years of his life were less eventful. Further inheritances had by now ended any threat of poverty. In many respects the Marxes' life now was like that of any comfortably-off bourgeois family: they moved to a larger house, spent a good deal on furnishing it, sent their children to a ladies' seminary, and travelled to fashionable Continental spas. Marx even claimed to have made money on the stock exchange – which did not stop him asking for, and receiving, further gifts of money from Engels.

Marx's ideas were spreading at last. By 1871 a second edition of *Capital* was needed. A Russian translation appeared in 1872 – Marx was very popular among Russian revolutionaries – and a French translation soon followed. Though *Capital* was not translated into English during Marx's lifetime (like his other books, it was written in German) Marx's growing reputation, even among the untheoretical English, was indicated by his inclusion in a series of pamphlets on 'Leaders in Modern Thought'. Marx and Engels kept up a correspondence with revolutionaries throughout Europe who shared their views. Otherwise Marx worked desultorily on the second and third volumes of *Capital*, but never got them ready for publication. This task was left to Engels after Marx's death. The last important work Marx wrote arose from a congress held in Gotha, in Germany, in 1875. The purpose of the congress was to unite rival German socialist parties, and to do this a common platform was drawn up. Neither Marx nor Engels was consulted about this platform – known as 'the Gotha Program' – and Marx was angry at the

3. The exterior of 41 Maitland Park Road, Haverstock Hill, London, where Marx spent the last fifteen years of his life

many deviations it contained from what he considered to be scientific socialism. He wrote a set of critical comments on the Program, and attempted to circulate it among German socialist leaders. After Marx's death this *Critique of the Gotha Program* was published and recognized as one of Marx's rare statements on the organization of a future communist society. At the time, however, Marx's critique had no influence, and the planned unification went ahead.

In his last years the satisfaction Marx might have gained from his growing reputation was overshadowed by personal sorrows. Marx's elder daughters, Jenny and Laura, married and had children, but none

4. Marx with his eldest daughter, Jenny, in 1870

of Laura's three children lived beyond the age of three. Jenny's firstborn also died in infancy, although she then had five more, all but one of whom survived to maturity. But in 1881 the older Jenny, Marx's dearly beloved wife, died after a long illness. Marx was now ill and lonely. In 1882 his daughter Jenny became seriously ill; she died in January 1883. Marx never got over this loss. He developed bronchitis and died on 14 March 1883.

Chapter 2
The Young Hegelian

Little more than a year after his arrival as a student in Berlin, Marx wrote to his father that he was now attaching himself 'ever more closely to the current philosophy'. This 'current philosophy' was the philosophy of G.W.F. Hegel, who had taught at the University of Berlin from 1818 until his death in 1831. Years later, Friedrich Engels described Hegel's influence in the period when he and Marx began to form their ideas:

> The Hegelian system covered an incomparably greater domain than any earlier system and developed in this domain a wealth of thought which is astounding even today . . .

> One can imagine what a tremendous effect this Hegelian system must have produced in the philosophy-tinged atmosphere of Germany. It was a triumphal procession which lasted for decades and which by no means came to a standstill on the death of Hegel. On the contrary, it was precisely from 1830 to 1840 that 'Hegelianism' reigned most exclusively, and to a greater or lesser extent infected even its opponents.

The close attachment to this philosophy Marx formed in 1837 was to affect his thought for the rest of his life. Writing about Hegel in 1844, Marx referred to *The Phenomenology of Mind* as 'the true birthplace and secret of his philosophy' (*EPM* 98). This long and obscure work is therefore the place to begin our understanding of Marx.

The German word for 'Mind' is sometimes translated as 'Spirit'. Hegel uses it to refer to the spiritual side of the universe, which appears in his writings as a kind of universal mind. My mind, your mind, and the minds of every other conscious being are particular, limited manifestations of this universal mind. There has been a good deal of debate about whether this universal mind is intended to be God or whether Hegel was, in pantheistic fashion, identifying God with the world as a whole. There is no definite answer to this question; but it seems appropriate and convenient to distinguish this universal mind from our own particular minds by writing the universal variety with a capital, as Mind.

The Phenomenology of Mind traces the development of Mind from its first appearance as individual minds, conscious but neither self-conscious nor free, to Mind as a free and fully self-conscious unity. The process is neither purely historical, nor purely logical, but a strange combination of the two. One might say that Hegel is trying to show that history is the progress of Mind along a logically necessary path, a path along which it must travel in order to reach its final goal.

The development of Mind is dialectical – a term that has come to be associated with Marx because his own philosophy has been referred to as 'dialectical materialism'. The dialectical elements of Marx's theory were taken over from Hegel, so this is a good place to see what 'dialectic' is.

Perhaps the most celebrated passage in the *Phenomenology* concerns the relationship of a master to a slave. It well illustrates what Hegel means by dialectic, and it introduces an idea echoed in Marx's view of the relationship between capitalist and worker.

Suppose we have two independent people, aware of their own independence, but not of their common nature as aspects of one universal Mind. Each sees the other as a rival, a limit to his own power over everything else. This situation is therefore unstable. A struggle ensues, in which one conquers and enslaves the other. The master/ slave relationship, however, is not stable either. Although it seems at first that the master is everything and the slave nothing, it is the slave who works and by his work changes the natural world. In this assertion of his own nature and consciousness over the natural world, the slave achieves satisfaction and develops his own self-consciousness, while the master becomes dependent on his slave. The ultimate outcome must therefore be the liberation of the slave, and the overcoming of the initial conflict between the two independent beings.

This is only one short section of the *Phenomenology*, the whole of which traces the development of Mind as it overcomes contradiction or opposition. Mind is inherently universal, but in its limited form, as the minds of particular people, it is not aware of its universal nature – that is, particular people do not see themselves as all part of the one universal Mind. Hegel describes this as a situation in which Mind is 'alienated' from itself – that is, people (who are manifestations of Mind) take other people (who are also manifestations of Mind) as something foreign, hostile, and external to themselves, whereas they are in fact all part of the same great whole.

Mind cannot be free in an alienated state, for in such a state it appears to encounter opposition and barriers to its own complete development. Since Mind is really infinite and all-encompassing, opposition and barriers are only appearances, the result of Mind not recognizing itself for what it is, but taking what is really a part of itself as something alien and hostile to itself. These apparently alien forces limit the freedom of Mind, for if Mind does not know its own infinite powers it cannot exercise these powers to organize the world in accordance with its plans.

The progress of the dialectical development of Mind in Hegel's

5. G. W. F. Hegel (1770–1831), whose philosophy provided the framework for Marx's ideas

philosophy is always progress towards freedom. 'The History of the World is none other than the progress of the consciousness of freedom,' he wrote. The *Phenomenology* is thus an immense philosophical epic, tracing the history of Mind from its first blind gropings in a hostile world to the moment when, in recognizing itself as master of the universe, it finally achieves self-knowledge and freedom.

Hegel's philosophy has an odd consequence which would have been embarrassing to a more modest author. If all history is the story of Mind working towards the goal of understanding its own nature, this goal is actually reached with the completion of the *Phenomenology* itself. When Mind, manifested in the mind of Hegel, grasps its own nature, the last stage of history has been reached.

To us this is preposterous. Hegel's speculative mixture of philosophy and history has been unfashionable for a long time. It was, however, taken seriously when Marx was young. Moreover we can make sense of much of the *Phenomenology* even if we reject the notion of a universal Mind as the ultimate reality of all things. We can treat 'Universal Mind' as a collective term for all human minds. We can then rewrite the *Phenomenology* in terms of the path to human liberation. The saga of Mind then becomes the saga of the human spirit.

This is what a group of philosophers known as Young Hegelians attempted in the decade following Hegel's death. The orthodox interpretation of Hegel was that since human society is the manifestation of Mind in the world, everything is right and rational as it is. There are plenty of passages in Hegel's works which can be quoted in support of this view. At times he seems to regard the Prussian state as the supreme incarnation of Mind. Since the Prussian state paid his salary as a professor of philosophy in Berlin, it is not surprising that the more radical Young Hegelians took the view that in these passages Hegel had betrayed his own philosophy. Among these was Marx, who wrote in his doctoral thesis: 'if a philosopher really has compromised, it is the job of his followers to use the inner core of his thought to illuminate his own superficial expressions of it' (D 13).

For the Young Hegelians the 'superficial expression' of Hegel's philosophy was his acceptance of the state of politics, religion, and society in early nineteenth-century Prussia: the 'inner core' was his account of Mind overcoming alienation, reinterpreted as an account of human self-consciousness freeing itself from the illusions that prevent it achieving self-understanding and freedom.

During his student days in Berlin and for a year or two afterwards Marx was close to Bruno Bauer, a lecturer in theology and a leading Young Hegelian. Under Bauer's influence Marx seized on orthodox religion as the chief illusion standing in the way of human self-understanding. The chief weapon against this illusion was philosophy. In the Preface to his doctoral thesis, Marx wrote:

> Philosophy makes no secret of it. The proclamation of Prometheus – in a word, I detest all the gods – is her own profession, her own slogan against all the gods of heaven and earth who do not recognize man's self-consciousness as the highest divinity. There shall be no other beside it.

> (D 12–13)

In accordance with the general method of the Young Hegelians, Bauer and Marx used Hegel's own critique of religion to reach more radical conclusions. In the *Phenomenology* Hegel referred to the Christian religion at a certain stage of its development as a form of alienation, for while God reigns in heaven, human beings inhabit an inferior and comparatively worthless 'vale of tears'. Human nature is divided between its essential nature, which is immortal and heavenly, and its non-essential nature, which is mortal and earthly. Thus individuals see their own essential nature as having its home in another realm; they are alienated from their mortal existence and the world in which they actually live.

Hegel, treating this as a passing phase in the self-alienation of Mind, drew no practical conclusions from it. Bauer reinterpreted it more broadly as indicating the self-alienation of human beings. It was humans, he maintained, who had created this God which now seemed to have an independent existence, an existence which made it impossible for humans to regard themselves as 'the highest divinity'. This philosophical conclusion pointed to a practical task: to criticize religion and show human beings that God is their own creation, thus ending the subordination of humanity to God and the alienation of human beings from their own true nature.

So the Young Hegelians thought Hegel's philosophy both mystifyingly presented and incomplete. When rewritten in terms of the real world instead of the mysterious world of Mind, it made sense. 'Mind' was read as 'human self-consciousness'. The goal of history became the liberation of humanity; but this could not be achieved until the religious illusion had been overcome.

Chapter 3
From God to Money

The transformation of Hegel's method into a weapon against religion
was carried through most thoroughly by another radical Hegelian,
Ludwig Feuerbach.

Friedrich Engels later wrote of the impact of the work that made
Feuerbach famous: 'Then came Feuerbach's *Essence of Christianity* . . .
One must himself have experienced the liberating effect of this book to
get an idea of it. Enthusiasm was general; we all became at once
Feuerbachians.' Like Bauer, Feuerbach in *The Essence of Christianity*
characterized religion as a form of alienation. God, he wrote, is to be
understood as the essence of the human species, externalized and
projected into an alien reality. Wisdom, love, benevolence – these are
really attributes of the human species, but we attribute them, in a
purified form, to God. The more we enrich our concept of God in this
way, however, the more we impoverish ourselves. The solution is to
realize that theology is a kind of misdescribed anthropology. What we
believe of God is really true of ourselves. Thus humanity can regain its
essence, which in religion it has lost.

When *The Essence of Christianity* appeared, in 1841, the first meeting
between Marx and Engels still lay two years ahead. The book may not
have made as much of an impression on Marx as it did on Engels, for
Marx had already been exposed to similar ideas through Bauer; but

Feuerbach's later works, particularly his *Preliminary Theses for the Reform of Philosophy,* did have a decisive impact on Marx, triggering off the next important stage in the development of his thought.

Feuerbach's later works went beyond the criticism of religion to the criticism of Hegelian philosophy itself. Yet it was a curious form of criticism of Hegel, for Feuerbach continued to work by transforming Hegel, using Hegel's method against all philosophy in the Hegelian mode. Hegel had taken Mind as the moving force in history, and humans as manifestations of Mind. This, according to Feuerbach, locates the essence of humanity outside human beings and thus, like religion, serves to alienate humanity from itself.

More generally, Hegel and other German philosophers of the idealist school began from such conceptions as Spirit, Mind, God, the Absolute, the Infinite, and so on, treating these as ultimately real, and regarding ordinary humans and animals, tables, sticks and stones, and the rest of the finite, material world as a limited, imperfect expression of the spiritual world. Feuerbach again reversed this, insisting that philosophy must begin with the finite, material world. Thought does not precede existence, existence precedes thought.

So Feuerbach put at the centre of his philosophy neither God nor thought, but man. Hegel's tale of the progress of Mind, overcoming alienation in order to achieve freedom, was for Feuerbach a mystifying expression of the progress of human beings overcoming the alienation of both religion and philosophy itself.

Marx seized on this idea of bringing Hegel down to earth by using Hegel's methods to attack the present condition of human beings. In his brief spell as editor of the *Rhenish Gazette*, Marx had descended from the rarefied air of Hegelian philosophy to more practical issues like censorship, divorce, a Prussian law prohibiting the gathering of dead timber from forests, and the economic distress of Moselle wine-growers. When the paper was suppressed Marx went back to philosophy, applying Feuerbach's technique of transformation to Hegel's political philosophy.

Marx's ideas at this stage (1843) are liberal rather than socialist, and he still thinks that a change in consciousness is all that is needed. In a letter to Arnold Ruge, a fellow Young Hegelian with whom he worked on the short-lived *German–French Annals,* Marx wrote: 'Freedom, the feeling of man's dignity, will have to be awakened again in these men. Only this feeling . . . can again transform society into a community of men to achieve their highest purposes, a democratic state.' And in a later letter to Ruge about their joint venture:

> we can express the aim of our periodical in one phrase: A self-understanding (equals critical philosophy) of the age concerning its struggles and wishes . . . To have its sins forgiven, mankind has only to declare them for what they are.

> (R 38)

Up to this point Marx had followed Feuerbach in reinterpreting Hegel as a philosopher of man rather than Mind. His view of human beings, however, focused on their mental aspect, their thoughts, and their consciousness. The first signs of a shift to his later emphasis on the material and economic conditions of human life came in an essay written in 1843 entitled 'On the Jewish Question'. The essay reviews two publications by Bruno Bauer on the issue of civil and political rights for Jews.

Marx rejects his friend's treatment of the issue as a question of religion. It is not the sabbath Jew we should consider, Marx says, but the everyday Jew. Accepting the common stereotype of Jews as obsessed with money and bargaining, Marx describes the Jew as merely a special manifestation of what he calls 'civil society's Judaism' – that is, the dominance in society of bargaining and financial interests

6. Marx in 1836, aged 18. Detail from the lithograph on p. 4

generally. Marx therefore suggests that the way to abolish the 'problem' of Judaism is to reorganize society so as to abolish bargaining.

The importance of this essay is that it sees economic life, not religion, as the chief form of human alienation. Another German writer, Moses Hess, had already developed Feuerbach's ideas in this direction, being the first, as Engels put it, to reach communism by 'the philosophic path'. (There had, of course, been many earlier communists who were more or less philosophical – what Engels meant was the path of Hegelian philosophy.) Now Marx was heading down the same route. The following quotation from 'On the Jewish Question' reads exactly like Bauer, Feuerbach, or Marx himself, a year or two earlier, denouncing religion – except that where they would have written 'God' Marx now substitutes 'money':

> Money is the universal, self-constituted value of all things. Hence it has robbed the whole world, the human world as well as nature, of its proper value. Money is the alienated essence of man's labour and life, and this alien essence dominates him as he worships it.

(J 60)

The final sentence points the way forward. First the Young Hegelians, including Bauer and Feuerbach, see religion as the alienated human essence, and seek to end this alienation by their critical studies of Christianity. Then Feuerbach goes beyond religion, arguing that any philosophy which concentrates on the mental rather than the material side of human nature is a form of alienation. Now Marx insists that it is neither religion nor philosophy, but *money* that is the barrier to human freedom. The obvious next step is a critical study of economics. This Marx now begins.

Before we follow this development, however, we must pause to note the emergence of another key element in Marx's work which, like economics, was to remain central to his thought and activity.

Chapter 4
Enter the Proletariat

We saw that when the Prussian government suppressed the newspaper he had been editing, Marx started work on a critique of Hegel's political philosophy. In 1844 he published, in the *German–French Annals,* an article entitled 'Towards a Critique of Hegel's *Philosophy of Right*: Introduction'. The critique which this article was to introduce remained unfinished, but the 'Introduction' stands alongside 'On the Jewish Question' as a milestone on the road to Marxism. For it is in this article that Marx first allocates to the working class a decisive role in the coming redemption of humanity.

The 'Introduction' starts by summarizing the attack on religion made by Bauer and Feuerbach. This passage is notable for its epigrams, including the frequently quoted description of religion as 'the opium of the people', but it says nothing new. Now that human self-alienation has been unmasked in its holy form, Marx continues, it is the task of philosophy to unmask it in its unholy forms, such as law and politics. He calls for more criticism of German conditions, to allow the German people 'not even a moment of self-deception'. But for the first time – and in contrast to Bauer and Feuerbach – Marx suggests that criticism by itself is not enough:

> The weapon of criticism obviously cannot replace the criticism of weapons. Material force must be overthrown by material force. But theory also becomes a material force once it has gripped the masses.
>
> (I 69)

In his initial recognition of the role of the masses, Marx treats this role as a special feature of the German situation, not applicable to France. Whereas in France 'every class of the nation is *politically idealistic* and experiences itself first of all not as a particular class but as representing the general needs of society', in Germany practical life is 'mindless' and no class can be free until it is forced to be by its *immediate* condition, by *material* necessity, by its *very chains*'. Where then, Marx asks, is the positive possibility of German freedom to be found? And he answers:

> In the formation of a class with *radical chains* ... a sphere of society having a universal character because of its universal suffering ... a sphere, in short, that is the *complete loss* of humanity and can only redeem itself through the *total redemption of humanity*. This dissolution of society as a particular class is the *proletariat*.

(I 72–3)

Marx concludes by placing the proletariat within the framework of a transformed Hegelian philosophy:

> As philosophy finds its material weapons in the proletariat, the proletariat finds its intellectual weapons in philosophy.

More explicitly:

> Philosophy cannot be actualized without the superseding of the proletariat, the proletariat cannot be superseded without the actualization of philosophy.

(I 73)

Here is the germ of a new solution to the problem of human alienation. Criticism and philosophical theory alone will not end it. A more practical force is needed, and that force is provided by the artificially impoverished working class. This lowest class of society will bring about 'the actualization of philosophy' – by which Marx means the culmination of the philosophical and historical saga described, in a mystified form, by Hegel. The proletariat, following the lead of the new radical philosophy, will complete the dialectical process in which humans have emerged, grown estranged from themselves, and become enslaved by their own alienated essence. Whereas the property-owning middle class could win freedom for themselves on the basis of rights to property – thus excluding others from the freedom they gain – the property-less working class possess nothing but their title as human beings. Thus they can liberate themselves only by liberating all humanity.

Before 1844, to judge from his writings, Marx scarcely noticed the existence of the proletariat; certainly he never suggested they had a part to play in overcoming alienation. Now, like a film director calling on the errand-boy to play Hamlet, Marx introduces the proletariat as the material force that will bring about the liberation of humanity. Why?

Marx did not arrive at his view of the proletariat as the result of detailed economic studies, for his economic studies were just beginning. He had read a great deal of history, but he does not buttress his position by quoting from historical sources, as he was later to do. His reasons for placing importance on the proletariat are philosophical rather than historical or economic. Since human alienation is not a problem of a particular class, but a universal problem, whatever is to solve it must have a universal character – and the proletariat, Marx claims, has this universal character in virtue of its total deprivation. It represents not a particular class of society, but all humanity.

That a situation should contain within itself the seed of its own dissolution, and that the greatest of all triumphs should come from the depths of despair – these are familiar themes in the dialectic of Hegel and his followers. (They echo, some have said, the redemption of humanity by the crucifixion of Jesus.) The proletariat fits neatly into this dialectical scenario, and one cannot help suspecting that Marx seized upon it precisely because it served his philosophical purposes so well.

To say this is not to say that when he wrote the 'Introduction' Marx knew nothing about the proletariat. He had just moved to Paris, where socialist ideas were much more advanced than in Germany. He mixed with socialist leaders of the time, living in the same house as one of the leaders of the League of the Just, a radical workers' group. His writings reflect his admiration of the French socialist workers: 'The nobility of man', he writes, 'shines forth from their toil-worn bodies' (MC 87). In giving so important a role to the proletariat, therefore, the 'Introduction' reflects a two-way process: Marx tailors his conception of the proletariat to suit his philosophy, and tailors his philosophy in accordance with his new-found enthusiasm for the working class and its revolutionary ideas.

Chapter 5
The First Marxism

Marx had now developed two important new insights: that economics is the chief form of human alienation, and that the material force needed to liberate humanity from its domination by economics is to be found in the working class. Up to this stage, however, he had only made these points briefly, in essays ostensibly on other topics. The next step was to use these insights as the basis of a new and systematic world-view, one which would transform and supplant the Hegelian system and all prior transformations of it.

Marx began his critical study of economics in 1844. It was to culminate in Marx's greatest work, *Capital*, the first volume of which was published in 1867, later volumes appearing after Marx's death. So the work Marx produced in Paris, known as the *Economic and Philosophic Manuscripts of 1844*, was the first version of a project that was to occupy him, in one form or another, for the rest of his life.

The 1844 version of Marxism was not published until 1932. The manuscript consists of a number of disconnected sections, some obviously incomplete. Nevertheless we can see what Marx was trying to do. He begins with a Preface which praises Feuerbach as the author of 'the only writings since Hegel's *Phenomenology* and *Logic* containing a real theoretical revolution'. There are then sections on the economics of wages, profits, and rent, in which Marx quotes liberally from the founding fathers of classical economics like J.-B. Say and Adam Smith. The point of this, as Marx explains, is to show that according to classical economics the worker becomes a commodity, the production of which is subject to the ordinary laws of supply and demand. If the supply of workers exceeds the demand for labour, wages fall and some workers starve. Wages therefore tend to the lowest possible level compatible with keeping an adequate supply of workers alive.

Marx draws another important point from the classical economists. Those who employ the workers – the capitalists – build up their wealth through the labour of their workers. They become wealthy by keeping for themselves a certain amount of the value their workers produce. Capital is nothing else but accumulated labour. The worker's labour increases the employer's capital. This increased capital is used to build bigger factories and buy more machines. This increases the division of labour. This puts more self-employed workers out of business. They must then sell their labour on the market. This intensifies the competition among workers trying to get work, and lowers wages.

All this Marx presents as deductions from the presuppositions of orthodox economics. Marx himself is not writing as an economist. He wants to rise above the level of the science of economics, which, he says, simply takes for granted such things as private property, greed, competition, and so on, saying nothing about the extent to which apparently accidental circumstances are really the expression of a necessary course of development. Marx wants to ask larger questions, ignored by economists, such as 'What in the evolution of mankind is the meaning of this reduction of the greater part of mankind to abstract labour?' (By 'abstract labour' Marx means work done simply in order to earn a wage, rather than for the worker's own specific purposes. Thus making a pair of shoes because one wants a pair of shoes is not abstract labour; making a pair of shoes because that happens to be a way of getting money is.) Marx, in other words, wants to give a deeper explanation of the meaning and significance of the laws of economics.

What type of explanation does Marx have in mind? The answer is apparent from the section of the manuscripts entitled 'Alienated Labour'. Here Marx explains the implications of economics in terms closely parallel to Feuerbach's critique of religion:

> The more the worker exerts himself, the more powerful becomes the alien objective world which he fashions against himself, the poorer he and his inner world become, the less there is that belongs to him. It is the same in religion. The more man attributes to God, the less he retains in himself. The worker puts his life into the object; then it no longer belongs to him but to the object . . . The externalization of the worker in his product means not only that his work becomes an object, an external existence, but also that it exists outside him, independently, alien, an autonomous power, opposed to him. The life he has given to the object confronts him as hostile and alien.
>
> (*EPM* 78–9)

The central point is more pithily stated in a sentence preserved in the notebooks Marx used when studying the classical economists, in preparation for the writing of the 1844 manuscripts:

> It is evident that economics establishes an alienated form of social intercourse as the essential, original and natural form.
>
> (M 116)

This is the gist of Marx's objection to classical economics. Marx does not challenge the classical economists within the presuppositions of their science. Instead he takes a viewpoint outside those presuppositions and argues that private property, competition, greed, and so on are to be found only in a particular condition of human existence, a condition of alienation. In contrast to Hegel, whom Marx

34

praises for grasping the self-development of man as a process, the classical economists take the present alienated condition of human society as its 'essential, original and definitive form'. They fail to see that it is a necessary but temporary stage in the evolution of mankind.

Marx then discusses the present alienated state of humanity. One of his premises is that 'man is a species-being'. The idea is taken directly from Feuerbach who in turn derived it from Hegel. Hegel, as we saw, told the story of human development in terms of the progress of a single Mind, of which individual human minds are particular manifestations. Feuerbach scrubbed out the super-Mind, and rewrote Hegel in less mysterious human terms; but he retained the idea that human beings are in some sense a unity. For Feuerbach the basis of this unity, and the essential difference between humans and animals, is the ability of humans to be conscious of their species. It is because they are conscious of their existence as a species that human beings can see themselves as individuals (that is, as one among others), and it is because humans see themselves as a species that human reason and human powers are unlimited. Human beings partake in perfection – which, according to Feuerbach, they mistakenly attribute to God instead of themselves – because they are part of a species.

Marx transforms Feuerbach, making the conception of man as a species-being still more concrete. For Marx 'Productive life . . . is species-life.' It is in activity, in production, that humans show themselves to be species-beings. The somewhat unconvincing reason Marx offers for this is that while animals produce only to satisfy their immediate needs, human beings can produce according to universal standards, free of any immediate need – for instance, in accordance with standards of beauty (*EPM* 82).

On this view, labour in the sense of free productive activity is the essence of human life. Whatever is produced in this way – a statue, a house, or a piece of cloth – is therefore the essence of human life made into a physical object. Marx calls this 'the objectification of man's species-life'. Ideally the objects workers have freely created would be theirs to keep or dispose of as they wish. When, under conditions of alienated labour, workers must produce objects over which they have no control (because the objects belong to the employers) and which are used against those who produced them (by increasing the wealth and power of the employers) the workers are alienated from their essential humanity.

A consequence of this alienation of humans from their own nature is that they are also alienated from each other. Productive activity becomes 'activity under the domination, coercion and yoke of another man'. This other man becomes an alien, hostile being. Instead of humans relating to each other co-operatively, they relate competitively. Love and trust are replaced by bargaining and exchange. Human beings cease to recognize in each other their common human nature; they see others as instruments for furthering their own egoistic interests.

That, in brief, is Marx's first critique of economics. Since in his view it is economic life rather than Mind or consciousness that is ultimately real, this critique is his account of what is really wrong with the present condition of humanity. The next question is: What can be done about it?

Marx rejects the idea that anything would be achieved by an enforced wage rise. Labour for wages is not free productive activity. It is merely a means to an end. Higher wages Marx describes as 'nothing but a better slave-salary'. It would not restore significance or dignity to workers or their labour. Even equal wages, as proposed by the French socialist Proudhon, would only replace individual capitalists with one overall capitalist, society itself (*EPM* 85).

The solution is the abolition of wages, alienated labour, and private property in one blow. In a word, communism. Marx introduces communism in terms befitting the closing chapter of a Hegelian epic:

> Communism . . . is the genuine resolution of the antagonism between man and nature and between man and man; it is the true resolution of the conflict between existence and essence, objectification and self-affirmation, freedom and necessity, individual and species. It is the riddle of history solved and knows itself as this solution.

(EPM 89)

One might expect that Marx would go on to explain in some detail what communism would be like. He does not – in fact nowhere in his writings does he give more than sketchy suggestions on this subject. He does, however, gesture at the enormous difference communism would make. All human senses, he claims, are degraded by private property. The dealer in minerals sees the market value of the jewels he handles, not their beauty. In the alienated condition caused by private property we cannot appreciate anything except by possessing it, or using it as a means. The abolition of private property will liberate our senses from this alienated condition, and enable us to appreciate the world in a truly human way just as the musical ear perceives a wealth of meaning and beauty where the unmusical ear can find none, so will the senses of social human beings differ from those of the unsocial.

These are the essential points of 'the first Marxism'. It is manifestly not a scientific enterprise in the sense in which we understand science today. Its theories are not derived from detailed factual studies, or subjected to controlled tests or observations.

The first Marxism is more down to earth than Hegel's philosophy of history, but it is a speculative philosophy of history rather than a scientific study. The aim of world history is human freedom. Human beings are not now free, for they are unable to organize the world so as to satisfy their needs and develop their human capacities. Private property, though a human creation, dominates and enslaves human beings. Ultimate liberation, however, is not in doubt; it is philosophically necessary. The immediate task of revolutionary theory is to understand in what way the present situation is a stage in the dialectical progress to liberation. Then it will be possible to encourage the movements that will end the present stage, ushering in the new age of freedom.

Marx's writings after 1844 – including all the works which made him famous – are reworkings, modifications, developments, and extensions of the themes of the *Economic and Philosophic Manuscripts*. The number and bulk of these writings make it impossible to discuss each work adequately. (Their repetitiveness would make it tedious, anyway.) So from here on I shall depart slightly from a strict chronological account. I shall begin by tracing the development of the materialist conception of history, which Marx himself described as the 'guiding thread for my studies' (P 389), and Engels, in his funeral oration by Marx's grave, hailed as Marx's chief discovery, comparable with Darwin's discovery of the theory of evolution. This will occupy the next two chapters. I shall then consider Marx's economic works, principally, of course, *Capital*. Since *Capital* was written only after Marx had arrived at the materialist conception of history, the departure from chronological order in this section will be slight. It will be greater in the next and last of these expository sections, which will assemble from passages of varying vintage Marx's thoughts on communism and on the ethical principles underlying his preference for a communist rather than a capitalist form of society.

Chapter 6
Alienation as a Theory of History

Marx's first published book – and, incidentally, the first work in which Engels participated – attacked articles published in the *General Literary Gazette* (*Allgemeine Literatur-Zeitung*), a journal edited by Marx's former friend and teacher, Bruno Bauer. Since Bauer's brother was a co-editor, the book was mockingly entitled *The Holy Family*. The best comment on it was made by Engels: 'the sovereign derision that we accord to the *General Literary Gazette* is in stark contrast to the considerable number of pages that we devote to its criticism'. Nevertheless some passages of *The Holy Family* are interesting because they show Marx in transition between the *Economic and Philosophic Manuscripts* and later statements of the materialist conception of history.

One section is a defence of the French socialist Proudhon and his objections to private property. Marx is still thinking in terms of alienation:

> The propertied class and the class of the proletariat represent the same human self-alienation. But the former feels comfortable and confirmed in this self-alienation, knowing that this alienation is its own power and possessing in it the semblance of a human existence. The latter feels itself ruined in this alienation and sees in it its impotence and the actuality of an inhuman existence.

Then comes a passage in which the outlines of an embryonic materialist theory of history are clearly visible:

> In its economic movement, private property is driven towards its own dissolution but only through a development which does not depend on it, of which it is unconscious, which takes place against its will, and which is brought about by the very nature of things – thereby creating the proletariat *as* proletariat, that spiritual and physical misery conscious of its misery, that dehumanization conscious of its dehumanization and thus transcending itself . . .

> It is not a question of what this or that proletarian or even the whole proletarian movement momentarily *imagines* to be the aim. It is a question of *what* the proletariat is and what it consequently is historically compelled to do. Its aim and historical action is prescribed, irrevocably and obviously, in its own situation in life as well as in the entire organization of contemporary civil society.

> (HF 134–5)

The structure of this and surrounding passages is Hegelian. Private property and the proletariat are described as 'antitheses' – the two sides of a Hegelian contradiction. It is a necessary contradiction, one which could not have been otherwise, for to maintain its own existence private property must also maintain the existence of the property-less working class needed to run the factories. The proletariat, on the other hand, is compelled to abolish itself on account of its miserable condition. This will require the abolition of private property. The end result will be that both private property and the proletariat 'disappear' in a new synthesis that resolves the contradiction.

Here we have an early version of the materialist theory of history. The basis of the dialectical movement Marx describes is the economic imperatives that flow from the existence of private property. The movement does not depend on the hopes and plans of people. The proletariat becomes conscious of its misery, and therefore seeks to overthrow capitalist society, but this consciousness arises only because of the situation of the proletariat in society. This is the point Marx and Engels were to make more explicitly in a famous passage of *The German Ideology*: 'Consciousness does not determine life, but life determines consciousness' (*GI* 164).

According to Engels' later account of the relationship between German philosophy and the materialist conception of history, 'the first document in which is deposited the brilliant germ of the new world outlook' is not *The Holy Family* but the 'Theses on Feuerbach' which Marx jotted down in the spring of 1845. These 'Theses' consist of eleven brief remarks in which Marx distinguishes his own form of materialism from that of Feuerbach. Because of their epigrammatic form they have become among the most quoted of Marx's writings. Because Engels published them in 1888, long before any of Marx's other early unpublished writings appeared, they are also among the most misunderstood.

Despite Engels' accolade, the 'Theses' largely recapitulate points Marx had made before. They attack Feuerbach and earlier materialists for taking a passive view of objects and our perception of them. Idealists like Hegel and Fichte emphasized that our activities shape the way we see the world. They were thinking of mental activity. A child sees a red ball, rather than a flat red circle, only when it has mentally grasped the idea of three-dimensional space. Marx wants to combine the active, dialectical side of idealist thought with the materialism of Feuerbach: hence 'dialectical materialism' as later Marxists called it (though Marx himself never used this phrase).

By the active side of materialism Marx meant practical human activity. Marx thought that practical activity was needed to solve theoretical problems. We have seen examples of this. In 'On the Jewish Question'

7. Ludwig Feuerbach (1804–72), who showed how Hegel's ideas could be transformed into a materialist philosophy and used to provide a radical critique of human alienation

Marx wrote that the problem of the status of Jews, which Bauer had seen as a problem in religious consciousness, would be abolished by reorganizing society so as to abolish bargaining. In 'Towards a Critique of Hegel's *Philosophy of Right*: Introduction', Marx argued that philosophy cannot be 'actualized' without the material weapon of the proletariat. And in the *Economic and Philosophic Manuscripts* Marx had referred to communism as 'the riddle of history solved'. This 'riddle of history' is, of course, a theoretical problem, a philosophical riddle. In Marx's transformation the contradictions of Hegelian philosophy become contradictions in the human condition. They are resolved by communism.

The 'Theses on Feuerbach' are the principal source of the celebrated Marxist doctrine of 'the unity of theory and practice'. This unity some think of as scribbling Marxist philosophy during quiet moments on the barricades. Others take it as meaning that one should live in accordance with one's theoretical principles – socialists sharing their wealth, for instance. The intellectual background of the 'Theses' makes it clear that Marx had neither of these ideas in mind. For Marx the unity of theory and practice meant the resolution of theoretical problems by practical activity. It is an idea which makes little sense outside the context of a materialist transformation of Hegel's philosophy of world history.

The eleventh thesis on Feuerbach is engraved on Marx's tombstone in Highgate Cemetery. It reads: 'The philosophers have only interpreted the world in various ways; the point is, to change it' (T 158). This is generally read as a statement to the effect that philosophy is unimportant; revolutionary activity is what matters. It means nothing of the sort. What Marx is saying is that the problems of philosophy cannot be solved by passive interpretation of the world as it is, but only by remoulding the world to resolve the philosophical contradictions inherent in it. It is to solve philosophical problems that we must change the world.

The materialist conception of history is a theory of world history in which practical human activity, rather than thought, plays the crucial role. The most detailed statement of the theory is to be found in Marx and Engels' next major work, *The German Ideology* (1846). Like *The Holy Family* this was a polemic of inordinate length against rival thinkers. Marx later wrote that the book was written 'to settle our accounts with our former philosophic conscience' (P 390).

This time Feuerbach is included in the criticism, although treated more respectfully than the others. It is in the section on Feuerbach that Marx and Engels take the opportunity to state their new view of world history:

> The first premise of all human history is, of course, the existence of living human individuals . . . Men can be distinguished from animals by consciousness, by religion, or by anything else you like. They themselves begin to distinguish themselves from animals as soon as they begin to produce their means of subsistence, a step which is conditioned by their physical organization. By producing means of subsistence men are indirectly producing their actual material life . . .

> In direct contrast to German philosophy, which descends from heaven to earth, here we ascend from earth to heaven. That is to say, we do not set out from what men say, imagine, conceive, nor from men as narrated, thought of, imagined, conceived, in order to arrive at men in the flesh. We set out from real, active men, and on the basis of their real life-process we demonstrate the development of the ideological reflexes and echoes of this life-process. The phantoms formed in the human brain are also, necessarily, sublimates of their material life-process, which is empirically verifiable and bound to material premises. Morality, religion, metaphysics and all the rest of ideology and their corresponding forms of consciousness no longer seem to be independent. They have no history or development. Rather, men who develop their material production and their material relationships alter

8. Friedrich Engels (1820–95), Marx's co-author, friend, benefactor, and the first Marxist

their thinking and the products of their thinking along with their real existence. Consciousness does not determine life, but life determines consciousness.

(*GI* 160, 164)

This is as clear a statement of the broad outline of his theory as Marx was ever to achieve. Thirteen years later, summing up the 'guiding thread' of his studies, he used similar language: 'It is not the consciousness of men that determines their existence, but, on the contrary, their social existence determines their consciousness'. With *The German Ideology* we have arrived at Marx's mature formulation of the outline of historical materialism (though not the detailed account of the process of change).

In view of this, and Marx's later description of the work as settling accounts with his 'former philosophic conscience', it might be thought that his early interest in alienation has now been replaced by a more scientific approach. It has not. Henceforth Marx makes more use of historical data and less use of abstract philosophical reasoning about the way the world must be; but his interest in alienation persists. *The German Ideology* still describes the social power as something which is really nothing other than the productive force of individuals, and yet appears to these individuals as 'alien and outside them' because they do not understand its origin and cannot control it. Instead of them directing it, it directs them. The abolition of private property and the regulation of production under communism would abolish this 'alienation between men and their products' and enable men to 'regain control of exchange, production and the mode of their mutual relationships' (*GI* 170).

It is not the use of the word 'alienation' that is important here. The same point can be made in other words. What is important is that Marx's theory of history is a vision of human beings in a state of alienation. Human beings cannot be free if they are subject to forces that determine their thoughts, their ideas, their very nature as human beings. The materialist conception of history tells us that human beings are totally subject to forces they do not understand and cannot control. Moreover the materialist conception of history tells us that these forces are not supernatural tyrants, for ever above and beyond human control, but the productive powers of human beings themselves. Human productive powers, instead of serving human beings, appear to them as alien and hostile forces. The description of this state of alienation is the materialist conception of history.

Chapter 7
The Goal of History

We have traced the development of the materialist conception of history from Marx's earlier concern with human freedom and alienation, but we have not examined the details of this theory of history. Is it really, as Engels claimed, a scientific discovery of 'the law of development of human history', comparable to Darwin's discovery of the law of development of organic nature?

The classic formulation of the materialist conception of history is that of the Preface to *A Contribution to the Critique of Political Economy*, written in 1859. We have already seen a little of this summary by Marx of his own ideas, but it merits a lengthier quotation:

> In the social production which men carry on they enter into definite relations that are indispensable and independent of their will; these relations of production correspond to a definite stage of development of their material powers of production. The sum total of these relations of production constitutes the economic structure of society – the real foundation, on which rise legal and political superstructures and to which correspond definite forms of social consciousness. The mode of production of material life conditions the general character of the social, political and spiritual processes of life. It is not the consciousness of men that determines their existence, but, on the contrary, their social existence determines their consciousness. At a certain stage of

their development the material forces of production in society come into conflict with the existing relations of production or – what is but a legal expression for the same thing – with the property relations within which they had been at work before. From forms of development of the forces of production these relations turn into their fetters. Then comes the epoch of social revolution. With the change of the economic foundation the entire immense superstructure is more or less rapidly transformed. In considering such transformations the distinction should always be made between the material transformation of the economic conditions of production, which can be determined with the precision of natural science, and the legal, political, religious, aesthetic, or philosophic – in short, ideological – forms in which men become conscious of this conflict and fight it out.

(P 389–90)

It is commonly said that Marx divided society into two elements, the 'economic base' and the 'superstructure', and maintained that the base governs the superstructure. A closer reading of the passage just quoted reveals a threefold, rather than a twofold, distinction. The opening sentence refers to relations of production, corresponding to a definite stage of the material powers of production. Thus we start with powers of production, or 'productive forces', as Marx usually calls them. The productive forces give rise to relations of production, and it is these relations – not the forces themselves – which constitute the economic structure of society. This economic structure, in turn, is the foundation on which the superstructure rises.

Marx's view may be clearer if made more specific. Productive forces are things used to produce. They include labour-power, raw materials, and the machines available to process them. If a miller uses a handmill to grind wheat into flour, the handmill is a productive force.

Relations of production are relations between people, or between people and things. The miller may own his mill, or may hire it from its owner. *Owning* and *hiring* are relations of production. Relations between people, such as 'Smith employs Jones' or 'Ramsbottom is the serf of the Earl of Warwick', are also relations of production.

So we start with productive forces. Marx says that relations of production correspond to the stage of development of productive forces. In one place he puts this very bluntly:

> The handmill gives you society with the feudal lord; the steam mill, society with the industrial capitalist.

> (PP 202)

In other words, when the productive forces are developed to the stage of manual power, the typical relation of production is that of lord and serf. This and similar relations make up the economic structure of society, which in turn is the foundation of the political and legal superstructure of feudal times, with the religion and morality that goes with it: an authoritarian religion, and a morality based on concepts of loyalty, obedience, and fulfilling the duties of one's station in life.

Feudal relations of production came about because they fostered the development of the productive forces of feudal times – the handmill for example. These productive forces continue to develop. The steam mill is invented. Feudal relations of production restrict the use of the steam mill. The most efficient use of steam power is in large factories which require a concentration of free labourers rather than serfs tied to their land. So the relation of lord and serf breaks down, to be replaced by the relation of capitalist and employee. These new relations of production constitute the economic structure of society, on which a capitalist legal and political superstructure rises, with its own religion and morality: freedom of religious conscience, freedom of contract, a right to disposable property, egoism, and competitiveness.

So we have a three-stage process: productive forces determine relations of production, which in turn determine the superstructure. The productive forces are fundamental. Their growth provides the momentum for the whole process of history.

But isn't all this much too crude? Should we take seriously the statement about the handmill giving us feudal lords, and the steam mill capitalists? Surely Marx must have realized that the invention of steam power itself depends on human ideas, and those ideas, as much as the steam mill itself, have produced capitalism. Isn't Marx making a deliberately exaggerated statement of his own position in order to display its novelty?

This is a vexed question. There are several other places where Marx says flatly that productive forces determine everything else. There are other statements which acknowledge the effect of factors belonging to the superstructure. Particularly when writing history himself, in *The Eighteenth Brumaire of Louis Bonaparte*, for instance, Marx traces the effects of ideas and personalities, and makes less deterministic general statements, for example:

> Men make their own history, but they do not make it just as they please; they do not make it under circumstances chosen by themselves, but under circumstances directly encountered, given, and transmitted from the past.
>
> (*EB* 300)

And what of the opening declaration of *The Communist Manifesto*: 'The history of all hitherto existing society is the history of class struggles'? If the forces of production control everything, class struggles can be no more than the superficial form in which these forces are cloaked. Like the images on a cinema screen they would be powerless to affect the underlying reality they reflect. So why describe history as the history of class struggles? And if neither thought nor politics has any real causal significance, what is the meaning of Marx's dedication, intellectually and politically, to the cause of the working class?

After Marx died, Engels denied that Marx had said that 'the economic element is the *only* determining one'. He and Marx, he conceded, were partly to blame for this misinterpretation, for they had emphasized the economic side in opposition to those who rejected it altogether. Marx and he had not, Engels wrote, overlooked the existence of interaction between the economic structure and the rest of the superstructure. They had affirmed only that 'the economic movement finally asserts itself as necessary'. According to Engels, Marx grew so irritated at misinterpretations of his doctrine that towards the end of his life, he declared: 'All I know is that I am not a Marxist.'

Was Engels right? Some have accused him of watering down the true doctrine; yet no one was in a better position to know what Marx really meant than his lifelong friend and collaborator. Moreover the relatively recent publication of Marx's *Grundrisse* – a rough preliminary version of *Capital* and other projects Marx never completed – reveals that Marx did, like Engels, use such phrases as 'in the last analysis' to describe the predominance of the forces of production in the interacting whole that constitutes human existence (*G* 495). Right or wrong, one cannot help sympathizing with Engels' position after Marx died. As the authoritative interpreter of Marx's ideas he had to present them in a plausible form, a form not refuted by common-sense observations about the effect of politics, religion, or law on the productive forces.

But once 'interaction' between the superstructure and the productive forces is admitted, is it still possible to maintain that production determines the superstructure, rather than the other way round? It is the old chicken-and-egg problem all over again. The productive forces determine the relations of production to which correspond the ideas of the society. These ideas lead to the further development of productive forces, which lead to new relations of production, to which correspond new ideas. In this cyclical movement it makes no more sense to say that productive forces play the determining role than to say that the egg ensures the continued existence of chickens rather than the other way round.

Talk of the productive forces 'finally' or 'in the last analysis' determining the other interacting factors does not provide a way out of the dilemma. For what can this mean? Does it mean that in the end the superstructure is totally governed by the development of the forces of production? In that case 'finally' merely stretches the causal chain; it is still a chain and so we are back with the hard-line determinist version of the theory.

On the other hand, if 'finally' not merely stretches, but actually breaks, the chain of economic determinism, it is difficult to see that asserting the primacy of the productive forces can mean anything significant at all. It might mean, as the passage from *The German Ideology* quoted in the previous chapter appears to suggest, that the process of human history only gets going when humans 'begin to produce their means of subsistence'; or as Engels put it in his graveside speech: 'mankind must first of all eat, drink, have shelter and clothing, before it can pursue politics, science, art, religion, etc.' But if politics, science, art, and religion, once they come into existence, have as much effect on the productive forces as the productive forces have on them, the fact that mankind must eat first and can only pursue politics afterwards is of historical interest only; it has no continuing causal importance.

Alternatively, describing the economic side as 'finally' asserting itself could be an attempt to say that although both economic and non-economic factors interact, a larger proportion of the causal impetus comes from the productive forces. But on what basis could one say this? How could one divide the interacting processes and say which

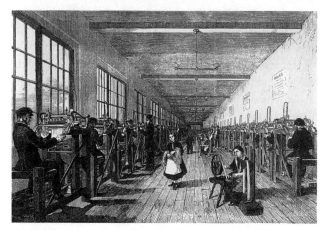

9. English factories in the mid-nineteenth century: men and women at work in the Patent Renewable Stocking Factory at Tewkesbury in 1860

played the larger role? We cannot solve the chicken-and-egg problem by saying that while the existence of the species is not due to the egg alone, the egg has more to do with it than the chicken.

In the absence of more plausible ways of making sense of the softening phrases used by Engels and – more rarely – Marx, the interpretation of the materialist conception of history seems to resolve itself into a choice between hard-line economic determinism, which would indeed be a momentous discovery if it were true, but does not seem to be true; or the much more pliable conception to be found in the *Grundrisse*, where Marx describes society as a 'totality', an 'organic whole' in which everything is interconnected (*G* 99–100). The view of society as a totality is no doubt illuminating when set against the view that ideas, politics, law, religion, and so on have a life and history of their own, independently of mundane economic matters. Nevertheless it does not amount to 'the law of development of human history', or to a scientific discovery comparable to Darwin's theory of evolution. To qualify as a contribution to science, a proposed law must be precise enough to enable us to deduce from it certain consequences rather than others. That is how we test proposed scientific laws – by seeing if the consequences they predict actually occur. The conception of society as an interconnected totality is about as precise an instrument of historical analysis as a bowl of porridge. Anything at all can be deduced from it. No observation could ever refute it.

It still needs to be explained how Marx, though obviously aware of the effect of the superstructure on the productive forces, could so confidently assert that the productive forces determine the relations of production and hence the social superstructure. Why did he not see the difficulty posed by the existence of interaction?

The explanation may be that belief in the primacy of the productive forces was not, for Marx, an ordinary belief about a matter of fact but a legacy of the origin of his theory in Hegelian philosophy.

One way to see this is to ask why, if Marx's view is inverted Hegelianism, the existence of interaction between ideas and material life does not pose exactly the same problem for Hegel's view (that the progress of Mind determines material life) as it poses for Marx's inversion of this view. Hegel's writings contain as many descriptions of material life influencing consciousness as Marx's contain of consciousness influencing material life. So the problem of establishing the primary causal role of one set of factors over the other should be as great for Hegel as for Marx.

Yet Hegel's reason for believing in the primacy of consciousness is clear: he regards Mind as ultimately real, and the material world as a manifestation of it; accordingly he sees the purpose or goal of history as the liberation of Mind from all illusions and fetters. Hegel's belief that consciousness determines material life therefore rests on his view

54

of ultimate reality and the meaning of history. History is not a chain of meaningless and often accidental occurrences, but a necessary process heading towards a discoverable goal. Whatever happens on the stage of world history happens in order to enable Mind to reach its goal. It is in this sense that what happens on the level of Mind, or consciousness, is the *real* cause of everything else.

Like Hegel, Marx has a view about what is ultimately real. His materialism is the reverse of Hegel's idealism. The materialist conception of history is usually regarded as a theory about the causes of historical change, rather than a theory about the nature of ultimate reality. In fact it is both – as Hegel's idealist conception of history was both. We have already seen passages from *The German Ideology* which indicate that Marx took material processes as real in a way that ideas are not. There Marx and Engels contrast the 'real life-process' of 'real, active men' with 'the ideological reflexes and echoes of this life-process'. They distinguish the 'phantoms formed in the human brain' from the 'material life-process, which is empirically verifiable'. The frequent reiteration of 'real' or 'actual' in describing the material or productive life of human beings, and the use of words like 'reflex', 'echo', 'phantom' and so on for aspects of consciousness, suggest a philosophical distinction between what is real and what is merely a manifestation or appearance.

Nor is this terminology restricted to Marx's early works. The contrast between appearance and reality is repeated in *Capital*, where the religious world is said to be 'but the reflex of the real world' (C I 79).

Also like Hegel, Marx thought that history is a necessary process heading towards a discoverable goal. We have seen evidence of this in the *Economic and Philosophic Manuscripts*, where Marx criticized classical economists for saying nothing about the meaning of economic phenomena 'in the evolution of mankind' or about the extent to which 'apparently accidental circumstances' are nothing but 'the expression of a necessary course of development'. That this too is not a view limited to Marx's youthful period seems clear from, for instance, the following paragraph from an article of his on British rule in India, written in 1853:

> England, it is true, in causing a social revolution in Hindustan, was actuated only by the vilest interests, and was stupid in her manner of enforcing them. But that is not the question. The question is, can mankind fulfil its destiny without a fundamental revolution in the social state of Asia? If not, whatever may have been the crimes of England, she was the unconscious tool of history in bringing about that revolution.

The references to 'mankind's destiny' and to England as 'the unconscious tool of history' imply that history moves in a purposive way towards some goal. (The whole paragraph is reminiscent of Hegel's account of how 'the cunning of reason' uses unsuspecting individuals to work its purposes in history.)

Marx's idea of the goal of world history was, of course, different from Hegel's. He replaced the liberation of Mind by the liberation of real human beings. The development of Mind through various forms of consciousness to final self-knowledge was replaced by the development of human productive forces, by which human beings free themselves from the tyranny of nature and fashion the world after their own plans. But for Marx the progress of human productive forces is no less necessary, and no less progress towards a goal, than the progress of Mind towards self-knowledge is for Hegel.

We can now explain the primary role of the productive forces in Marx's theory of history in the same manner as we explained Hegel's opposite conviction: for Marx the productive life of human beings, rather than their ideas and consciousness, is ultimately real. The development of these productive forces, and the liberation of human capacities that this development will bring, is the goal of history.

Marx's suggestion about England's role in advancing mankind towards its destiny illustrates the nature of the primacy of material life. Since England's colonial policy involves a series of political acts, the causing of a social revolution in Asia by this policy is an instance of the superstructure affecting the economic base. This happens, though, in order to develop the productive forces to the state necessary for the fulfilment of human destiny. The superstructure acts only as the 'unconscious tool' of history. England's colonial policy is no more the ultimate cause of the social revolution in Asia than my spade is the ultimate cause of the growth of my vegetables.

If this interpretation is correct the materialist theory of history is no ordinary causal theory. Few historians – or philosophers for that matter – now see any purpose or goal in history. They do not explain history as the necessary path to anywhere. They explain it by showing how one set of events brought about another. Marx, in contrast, saw history as the progress of the real nature of human beings, that is, human beings satisfying their wants and exerting their control over nature by their productive activities. The materialist conception of history was not conceived as a modern scientific account of how economic changes lead to changes in other areas of society. It was conceived as an explanation of history which points to the real forces operating in it, and the goal to which these forces are heading.

That is why, while recognizing the effect of politics, law, and ideas on the productive forces, Marx was in no doubt that the development of the productive forces determines everything else. This also makes sense of Marx's dedication to the cause of the working class. Marx was acting as the tool – a fully conscious tool – of history. The productive forces always finally assert themselves, but they do so through the actions of individual humans who may or may not be conscious of the role they are playing in history.

Chapter 8
Economics

Although Marx described the materialist conception of history as the leading thread of his studies, he was in no doubt that his masterpiece was *Capital*. In this book he presented his economic theories to the public in their most finished form. 'Most finished', not 'finished'; Marx saw only the first volume of *Capital* through to publication. The second and third volumes were published by Engels, and a fourth volume, entitled *Theories of Surplus Value*, by the German socialist Kautsky.

As with the materialist conception of history, so with the economics: the mature form is easier to appreciate in the light of earlier writings. So let us return to Marx's ideas in 1844, the point at which we ceased to follow their general development and went off in pursuit of the materialist conception of history.

By 1844 Marx had come to hold that the capitalist economic system, regarded by the classical economists as natural and inevitable, was an alienated form of human life. Under capitalism workers are forced to sell their labour – which Marx regards as the essence of human existence – to the capitalists, who use this labour to accumulate more capital, which further increases the power of the capitalists over the workers. Capitalists become rich, while wages are driven down to the bare minimum needed to keep the workers alive. Yet in reducing so large a class of people to this degraded condition, capitalism creates the material force that will overthrow it. For Marx, the importance of economics lay in the insight it provided into the workings of this alienation and the manner in which it could be overcome.

In the years immediately after 1844 Marx's major literary efforts went into polemical works: *The Holy Family*, *The German Ideology,* and *The Poverty of Philosophy*. In the course of castigating his opponents Marx developed the materialist conception of history, but did not greatly advance his economic theories. His first attempt to work out these theories in any detail came in 1847, when he gave a series of lectures on economics to the Workingmen's Club in Brussels. The lectures were revised and published as newspaper articles in 1849, and later reprinted under the title *Wage Labour and Capital*.

Wage Labour and Capital is a lucidly written work, containing many echoes of the 1844 manuscripts, but without their Hegelian terminology. It is worth examining in some detail, because its clarity makes the more difficult *Capital* easier to grasp.

Marx starts with labour. Labour is described as 'the worker's own life-activity, the manifestation of his own life'. Yet it becomes, under capitalism, a commodity the worker must sell in order to live. Therefore his life-activity is reduced to a means to go on living, not part of his life, but 'a sacrifice of his life'. His real life only begins when his work ceases, 'at table, in the public house, in bed' (*WLC* 250).

Marx then asks how wages are determined and answers that the price of labour is determined like the price of any other commodity. It may rise or fall according to supply and demand, but the general tendency is for wages to level down to the cost of production of labour, that is, the cost necessary for keeping the worker alive and capable of working and reproducing.

Next Marx turns to capital. He states the view of classical economics, that capital consists of the raw materials, instruments of production, and means of subsistence which are used in further production. Since all these elements of capital are the creation of labour, even the classical economists hold that capital is accumulated labour.

What the classical economists overlook, however, is that all this is true only within a certain set of social relations. Just as a Negro is not, as such, a slave, but can become a slave in a slave-owning society, so accumulated labour becomes capital only in bourgeois society.

The classical economists see capital as natural, rather than socially conditioned, because they see it as material products – machines, raw materials, etc. These material products, however, are also commodities. Commodities are items which can be exchanged against other items – for instance, a pound of sugar may be exchangeable for two pounds of potatoes, or half a pound of strawberries. They therefore have exchange-value. 'Exchange-value' is a key term in Marxist economics. It is contrasted with 'use-value'. The use-value of a pound of sugar is its power to satisfy people's desires for something sweet. The exchange-value of a pound of sugar is two pounds of potatoes or, expressed in terms of money, say, 20p. Use-values therefore exist independently of a market or any other system of exchange: exchange-values do not.

Now capital is really a sum of commodities, that is, of exchange-values. Whether it consists of wool, cotton, machines, buildings, or ships, it remains capital.

While all capital is a sum of exchange-values, however, not all sums of exchange-values are capital. A sum of exchange-values becomes capital only if used to increase itself by being exchanged for labour. Thus capital cannot exist without hiring wage labour. Nor can wage labour exist unless hired by capital. This is the basis of the claim made by bourgeois economists that the interests of the capitalists and the workers are one and the same.

Marx now examines this 'much-vaunted community of interests between worker and capitalist'. He takes the case most favourable for the bourgeois economists, the situation in which capital is growing, and hence the demand for labour, and the price of labour, is rising.

Marx's first point is one still made by critics of the modern consumer society:

> A house may be large or small; as long as the surrounding houses are equally small it satisfies all social demands for a dwelling. But let a palace arise beside the little house, and it shrinks from a little house to a hut . . . however high it may shoot up in the course of civilization, if the neighbouring palace grows to an equal or even greater extent, the occupant of the relatively small house will feel more and more uncomfortable, dissatisfied and cramped within its four walls.
>
> (*WLC* 259)

The reason for poverty and affluence being relative to the standard of our neighbours is, Marx says, that our desires are of a social nature. They are produced by our life in society, rather than by the objects we desire themselves. Thus rising wages do not produce greater satisfaction if the standard of living of the capitalist has risen even more. Yet this is exactly what happens when the growth of capital produces a rise in wages. Growth in capital means a growth in profit, but Marx, following the classical economist Ricardo, claims this can only happen if the relative share of wages is reduced. Wages may rise in real terms, but the gulf between workers and capitalists will increase.

There is also a more fundamental opposition between capitalists and workers. If capital grows, the domination of capital over workers increases. Wage labour 'produces the wealth that rules over it', and gets from this hostile power its means of subsistence, only on condition that it again assists the growth of capital.

Capital increases its domination by increasing the division of labour. This occurs because competition between capitalists forces them to make labour ever more productive, and the greater the scale on which they can produce, and the greater the division of labour, the more productive labour is. The increasing division of labour has several effects.

First, it enables one worker to do the work of ten, and so increases the competition among workers for jobs, thus driving wages down.

Second, it simplifies labour, eliminates the special skills of the worker and transforms him into 'a simple, monotonous productive force'.

Third, it puts more small-scale capitalists out of business. They can do nothing but join the working class. 'Thus', says Marx, 'the forest of uplifted arms demanding work becomes ever thicker, while the arms themselves become ever thinner.'

Finally, Marx says, as the scale of production increases and new markets are needed to dispose of the production, economic crises become more violent. Initially a crisis of overproduction can be relieved by opening up a new market or more thoroughly exploiting an old one. This room for manoeuvre shrinks as production expands, and *Wage Labour and Capital* closes with an image of capitalism collapsing into its grave, but taking with it the corpses of its slaves, the workers, who perish in economic crises.

And all this, Marx ironically reminds us, when capital is growing – the most favourable condition for wage labour!

Wage Labour and Capital contains no answer to a crucial puzzle common to classical economists like David Ricardo and Marx in his own early theory. Both held that commodities are, on average, exchanged for their value. They also held a 'labour theory of value', namely the theory that the exchange-value of a commodity corresponds to the amount of labour it takes to produce it. (Value is, Marx was later to write, 'crystallized social labour' (WPP 379).) But labour is a commodity too. Like other commodities, it should, on average, be exchanged for its value. The capitalist who buys a day's labour should therefore, on average, have to pay the value of a day's labour. This will add the value of a day's labour to the production cost of the commodity the worker produces in that day. This commodity the capitalist will then sell for a price that, on average, corresponds to the value of the labour required to produce it. Where then does the capitalist get his profit from?

Marx first worked out his solution to this puzzle in unpublished notebooks written in 1857–8. These notebooks contain, in draft form, a good deal of material that was to appear in *Capital*, but the four fat volumes of *Capital* appear to be only a portion of the works projected in the notebooks. The notebooks were published only in 1953 and not translated into English until 1972. They are known as the *Grundrisse*, a German word meaning 'outlines' or 'foundations', since they were first published, in German, under the title *Foundations of the Critique of Political Economy (Rough Draft)*.

The most intriguing point about the *Grundrisse* is that although it was written well into Marx's maturity, it is closer, in both terminology and method of argument, to the 1844 *Manuscripts* than to any of the works published in Marx's lifetime after 1844. Even if it were not possible to trace transformed Hegelian themes in Marx's mature published works, the *Grundrisse* makes it plain that Marx did not make the decisive break with Hegelian philosophy that his reference to *The German Ideology* as

10. David Ricardo (1772–1823), the English political economist whose labour theory of value greatly influenced Marx

'settling accounts with our former philosophic conscience' has been taken to imply.

The key element of Marx's mature economic theory appears in the *Grundrisse*. The worker, Marx writes,

> sells labour itself as *objectified labour*; i.e. he sells labour only in so far as it already objectifies a definite amount of labour, hence in so far as its equivalent is already measured, given; capital buys it as living labour as the general productive force of wealth; activity which increases wealth.
>
> (*G* 307)

What does Marx mean by this distinction between objectified labour and living labour? Objectified labour is the predetermined amount for which the capitalist pays – for instance, the worker's labour for twelve hours. This is labour as a commodity. The exchange-value of this commodity is the amount needed to produce it, that is, the amount needed to keep the worker alive and reproductive. But there is a dual nature to the exchange of labour and capital. The capitalist obtains the use of the worker's labour-power for the prescribed period – say, one day – and can use this labour-power to produce as much wealth as he is able to get out of it. This is what Marx means when he says that capital buys 'living labour'. The worker gets a fixed sum, regardless of what the capitalist can make out of his labour-power.

Here we have what Engels in his funeral oration described as the second of Marx's great discoveries: 'the discovery of surplus value'. Surplus value is the value the capitalist is able to extract from the labour-power he buys, above the exchange-value of the labour that he must pay. It is the difference between labour-power as a creative, productive force, and labour-time as an objectified commodity.

Suppose that the cost of keeping a worker alive and reproducing for one day is £1, and suppose that a day's work consists of twelve hours.

Then the exchange-value of twelve hours' labour will be £1. Fluctuations above this figure will be short-lived. Suppose, however, that the development of the forces of production means that a worker's labour-power can be used to add £1 to the value of some raw materials in only six hours. Then the worker effectively earns his wages in six hours. But the capitalist has bought twelve hours of labour-power for his £1, and can now use the remaining six hours to extract surplus value from the worker. This is, Marx claims, the secret of how capital is able to use the worker's creative power to increase its domination over the worker.

Marx published some of his new economic ideas in 1859, in *A Contribution to the Critique of Political Economy*. This work is justifiably famous for the succinct summary of the materialist view of history contained in its Preface, which we have already discussed; but the economic ideas were insignificant compared with those published eight years later in the first volume of *Capital*. So we shall go straight on to this pinnacle of Marx's writings.

Capital has a familiar-sounding subtitle – *Critique of Political Economy* – and once again the work criticizes classical economic theories, both within their own presuppositions and from a broader point of view. But *Capital* also contains historical material on the origin of capital, and detailed descriptions, drawn from government publications like the reports of factory inspectors, of the horrific nature of factory labour. We can see how all this fits in with Marx's general theoretical system by examining the first chapter of *Capital*, on commodities, and particularly the final section of this chapter, intriguingly entitled 'The Fetishism of Commodities and the Secret thereof'.

According to Marx, commodities are mysterious things in which the social character of human labour appears to be an objective feature of the product of that labour. He illustrates this with religion. In religion, Marx says, the productions of the human brain seem to be independent beings. Similarly, with commodities, a social relation between human beings appears in the form of the value of a commodity, as if that value were objective and independent of human relations. Like religious believers bowing before an idol, we make a fetish of commodities by treating them as more than they really are.

How does this happen? It happens only when we begin to produce things not because they directly serve our wants, but in order to exchange them. Since the exchange-value of a product corresponds to the amount of labour required to produce it, when we produce in order to exchange, the value of our labour becomes its exchange-value, rather than its use-value. When we exchange our products we are, without being aware of it, taking as equal the different kinds of labour embedded in them.

In a society based on the production of commodities there is, Marx says, a 'mystical veil' over these 'life-processes of society' which would not exist if we produced 'as freely associated men', consciously regulating our production in a planned way. Then the value of a product would be its use-value, the extent to which it satisfies our desires. Classical economists like Adam Smith and David Ricardo lifted the veil far enough to see that the value of a product (i.e. its exchange-value) represents the labour-time it took to produce it; but they took this as a law of nature, a self-evident necessary truth. On the contrary, says Marx, it bears the stamp of a society 'in which the process of production has the mastery over man, instead of being controlled by him'.

The aim of *Capital*, then, is to rip aside this mystical veil over the life-processes of modern society, revealing these processes as the domination of human beings by their own social relations. Thus *Capital*, like Marx's other writings, is based on the idea that human beings are in a state of alienation, a state in which their own creations appear to them as alien, hostile forces and in which instead of controlling their creations, they are controlled by them.

11. The round reading room of the old British Library, opened in 1842, where Marx worked on *Das Kapital*

Within this overall conception, the detail of *Capital* falls into place. The economic theory, contained mostly in the first nine chapters, is an attempt to display the real economic basis of production in a capitalist society. Here Marx debates with the classical economists, trying to show that, even on their own terms, he has a better account of the economic workings of capitalism.

Most of these first nine chapters prepare the ground for, and then introduce, the notion of surplus value. This involves a lengthy re-statement, in plain language, of the point made in more Hegelian terms in the *Grundrisse*. The dual nature of commodities, which can be seen as use-values or exchange-values, affects labour too. What is special about labour, though, is that it is the measure of exchange-value. Thus a new machine which makes it possible to produce two coats in the time it used to take to produce one will increase the use-value of an hour's labour (because two coats are more useful than one) but will not increase the exchange-value of the hour's labour (because an hour's labour remains an hour's labour, and if a coat only takes half as long to make as it used to, it will, in the end, be worth correspondingly less). Increasing the fruitfulness of labour therefore increases its use-value but not the exchange-value of its output.

This is how capitalism enslaves its workers. Through machinery and the division of labour, capitalism greatly increases the productivity of human labour; but this increased productivity does not benefit the producers. If in pre-capitalist times people had to work for twelve hours to produce the necessities of life, doubling the productivity of their labour ought to mean that they can now choose between an extra six hours of leisure, twice as many useful products, or some combination of the two. Under capitalism, however, labour is geared to the production of goods for exchange. Paradoxically, under these conditions increased productivity does not lead to the production of more exchange-value. Instead, the exchange-value per item of what is produced drops. Small independent producers are forced to become wage-labourers, since they cannot produce as many items in a day as the larger producers who obtain economies of scale by the use of wage-labourers. Since wages tend to fall to the level at which they barely sustain the labouring class, the overwhelming majority of human beings have lost, not gained, by the increased productivity of human labour. That, at any rate, is Marx's view.

But what happens to the increased productivity, if it does not improve the lives of the workers? Marx's answer is that it is skimmed off from the worker's output in the form of surplus value. The capitalist obtains the use-value of the worker's labour-power, and pays only the exchange-value. Because labour-power is a commodity which can be used to produce more value than it has itself, the capitalist is able to retain the difference between the two.

The fact that the worker obtains only the exchange-value, rather than the use-value, of his labour, means that in order to earn enough to support himself he has to work a full day – say, twelve hours – whereas his labour produces the use-values of the necessary food, clothing, shelter, and so on in, say, six hours. The six hours in which the worker produces the value of the goods he needs Marx calls 'necessary labour' because it is labour that the worker would have to undertake in any economic system, given the level of development of forces of production; but the extra six hours are surplus-labour, which is in effect a form of forced labour for the benefit of the capitalist. The essential difference between a society based on slave-labour and one based on wage-labour lies, Marx says, only in the manner in which this surplus-labour is extracted from the real producer, the worker.

The significance of all this lies in the fact that Marx regards the period in which people must work to keep themselves alive as a period in which they are not free:

> The realm of freedom actually begins only where labour which is determined by necessity and mundane considerations ceases.
>
> (C III 496)

In primitive societies property was held in common. People were not alienated from each other, or from the products of their labour, but at the same time human productive forces were so poorly developed that people had to spend much of their time providing for their needs, and for all that time were not free to choose what to do. The growth of the forces of production led to a feudal form of society in which the serf was subordinate to the feudal lord, and had to work a specified number of days on the lord's land rather than on his own. It was then perfectly obvious when the serf was working to feed himself and when he was working for his lord. At neither time was he free to choose his own activity.

The vastly greater development of productive forces that takes place under capitalism provides the means, Marx believes, to reduce the domination of nature over us to insignificant proportions and increase human freedom proportionately; but this cannot take place under capitalism, because the forced labour of the serf for the feudal lord still exists as the forced labour of the worker for the capitalist. The difference is that under feudalism the nature and extent of the forced labour is apparent; under capitalism the nature and extent of the coercion is disguised. Workers appear to be 'free labourers', voluntarily making agreements with capitalists. In fact the position of workers as a class in relation to capitalists as a class means that they are not free. They must take the terms the capitalists offer them, or starve; and capitalists will only employ them under terms which allow surplus-value to be extracted from their labour. This is not because capitalists are cruel or greedy – though some may be – but because of the economic laws inherent in capitalist production which, through free competition, coerce individual capitalists as much as individual workers. (Though equally coerced, capitalists suffer less from this coercion than workers.)

Marx sums all this up as the development of capitalism into:

> a coercive relation, which compels the working class to do more work than the narrow round of its own life-wants prescribes. As a producer of the activity of others, as a pumper-out of surplus-labour and exploiter of labour-power, it surpasses in energy, disregard of bounds, recklessness and efficiency, all earlier systems of production based on directly compulsory labour.
>
> (C I 310)

The most gripping chapters of *Capital* are not those in which Marx expounds his economic theories, but those which record the consequences of capitalist efficiency. The tenth chapter, on 'The Working Day', chronicles the capitalists' attempts to squeeze more and more labour-time out of the workers, oblivious of the human costs of working seven-year-old children for fifteen hours a day. The struggle for a legally limited working day is, Marx writes, more vital to the working classes than a pompous catalogue of 'the inalienable rights of man' (C I 302). Other chapters describe how the increasing division of labour eliminates intellectual and manual skill and reduces the labourer to a mere appendage to a machine; how industrialization has ruined cottage industries, forcing hand-workers to starve; how capitalism creates an 'industrial reserve army' of unemployed workers, subsisting in the direst poverty, to keep the 'active labour-army' in check; and how the agricultural population of England had their land taken from them by landlords and capitalists, so that they could survive only by selling their labour-power. The documented evidence presented justifies Marx's description of capital as 'dripping from head to foot, from every pore, with blood and dirt' (C I 760).

Near the end of the first volume of *Capital* the gloom lifts. Marx sketches how the laws of capitalism will bring about the destruction of capitalism. On the one hand competition between capitalists will lead to an ever-diminishing number of monopoly capitalists: on the other hand the 'misery, oppression, slavery, degradation, exploitation' of the working class grows (C I 763). But the working class is, because of the nature of capitalist production, more numerous and better organized. Eventually the dam will burst. The ensuing revolution will be, says Marx, lapsing into the style of his earlier writings, 'the negation of the negation'. It will not mean a return to private property in the old sense, but to property based on the gains made under capitalism, that is, on co-operation and common possession of land and the means of production. Capitalism will make the transition relatively easy, since it has already expropriated all private property into its own hands. All that is now necessary is for the mass of the people to expropriate these few expropriators.

The second and third volumes of *Capital* are much less interesting than the first. The second volume is a technical discussion of how capital circulates. It also discusses the origin of economic crises. The third volume attempts to patch up some problems in the first volume, particularly the objection that prices do not reflect the amount of labour in a product, as one would expect them to do on Marx's account. More important is Marx's claim that under capitalism the rate of profit tends to fall. Marx argued that the surplus-value of the past accumulates in the form of capital. Hence capital is always increasing, and the ratio of 'living labour' to capital is always decreasing; but since capitalists only make profit by extracting surplus-value from living labour, this means that the rate of profit must fall in the long run. All this was part of Marx's attempt to show that capitalism cannot be a permanent state of society.

Marx, Engels, and later Marxists treat *Capital* as a contribution to the science of economics. Taken in this way it is open to several objections. For instance, Marx asserts that all profit arises from the extraction of

Das Kapital.

Kritik der politischen Oekonomie.

Von

Karl Marx.

Erster Band.

Buch I: Der Produktionsprocess des Kapitals.

Hamburg

Verlag von Otto Meissner.

1867.

New-York: L. W. Schmidt, 24 Barclay-Street.

12. Cover of the first German edition of *Das Kapital*, vol. 1

surplus-value from living labour; machines, raw materials, and other forms of capital cannot generate profit, though they can increase the amount of surplus-value extracted. This seems obviously wrong. Future capitalists will not find their profits drying up as they dismiss the last workers from their newly automated factories. Many of Marx's other theories have been refuted by events: the theory that wages will always tend downwards to the subsistence level of the workers; the theory of the falling rate of profit; the theory that under capitalism economic crises will become more and more severe; the theory that capitalism requires an 'industrial reserve army' of paupers; and the theory that capitalism will force more and more people down into the working class.

Does this mean that the central theses of *Capital* are simply mistaken, and that the work is just another piece of crackpot economics – as we might have expected from a German philosopher meddling in a field in which he has not been trained? If this view seems at all plausible, Marx himself, with his emphasis on the scientific nature of his discovery, must bear the blame. It would be better to regard *Capital*, not as the work of 'a minor post-Ricardian' (as a leading contemporary economist has appraised Marx as an economist) but as the work of a critic of capitalist society. Marx wanted to expose the deficiencies of classical economics in order to expose the deficiencies of capitalism. He wanted to show why the enormous increase in productivity brought about by the industrial revolution had made the great majority of human beings worse off than before. He wanted to reveal how the old relationships of master and slave, lord and serf, survived under the cloak of freedom of contract. His answer to these questions was the doctrine of surplus-value. As an economic doctrine it does not stand up to scientific probing. Marx's economic theories are not a scientific account of the nature and extent of exploitation under capitalism. They nevertheless offer a vivid picture of an uncontrolled society in which the productive workers unconsciously create the instruments of their own oppression. It is a picture of human alienation, writ large as the dominance of past labour, or capital, over living labour. The value of the picture lies in its capacity to lead us to see its subject in a radically new way. It is a work of art, of philosophical reflection and of social polemic, all in one, and it has the merits and the defects of all three of these forms of writing. It is a painting of capitalism, not a photograph.

Chapter 9
Communism

In his speech at Marx's funeral, Engels said that although the materialist conception of history and the doctrine of surplus value were Marx's crowning theoretical discoveries

> Marx was before all else a revolutionist. His real mission in life was to contribute, in one way or another, to the overthrow of capitalist society and of the state institutions which it had brought into being, to contribute to the liberation of the modern proletariat . . .

To complete our account of Marx's main ideas, therefore, we need to ask: what kind of society did Marx hope would take the place of capitalism? This question is easily answered in a single word: communism. It is difficult to answer it more adequately, that is, to say what Marx meant by communism.

There is a reason for Marx's reticence over the details of communist society. He believed that history owed its momentum to the development of the forces of production rather than the development of ideas. This did not mean that theory was unimportant. If Marx's mission in life was to contribute to the overthrow of capitalism and the liberation of the proletariat, his theories of history and of economics were intended to do this by showing the workers their role in history and making them conscious of the manner in which capitalism exploited them. While theory could describe existing reality in this way, however, for theory to reach ahead of its time was another matter altogether. Marx derided as 'Utopian' those socialists who sought to bring about communism by producing blueprints of a future communist society. His own form of socialism was, he claimed, scientific because it built on knowledge of the laws of history that would bring socialism into existence.

Along with Utopian views of socialism, and for the same reason, Marx condemned conspiratorial revolutionaries who wished to capture power and introduce socialism before the economic base of society had developed to the point at which the working class as a whole is ready to participate in the revolution. Utopian dreamers and revolutionary conspirators fancy that the laws of history will bend to their desires. Marx prided himself on his freedom from this illusion. He saw his role as raising the revolutionary consciousness of the workers and preparing for the revolution that would occur when conditions were ripe. He thought he could describe the underlying laws governing the past and his own time, but he knew he could not impose his own will on the course of history. Nor could he predict the form to be taken by the new society to be built by the free human beings of the new era.

That, at least, was Marx's official position. In practice he could not refrain entirely from hinting at the form communist society would take.

We have seen that in his first discussion, in the *Economic and Philosophic Manuscripts of 1844*, Marx described communism as 'the riddle of history solved' and as the resolution of various conflicts that have existed throughout all previous history: the conflicts between man and nature, between man and man, between freedom and necessity, and between individual and species. This conception of communism is thoroughly Utopian – though not in Marx's sense of the word. It sees communism as the goal of history and the answer to all problems, as a virtual paradise on earth.

A similarly Utopian conception of communism can be found in *The German Ideology*, where Marx suggests that in communist society the division of labour would not force us into narrow occupational roles. I could, Marx says, 'hunt in the morning, fish in the afternoon, breed cattle in the evening, criticize after dinner, just as I like, without ever becoming a hunter, a fisherman, a herdsman, or a critic' (*GI* 169). More important than this idyllic image of pastoral communism, however, is Marx's claim in the same passage that the split between the particular interests of the individual and the common interest of society would disappear under communism. This is in line with his earlier remarks about communism resolving such conflicts as that between man and man, and between the individual and the species. It is crucial to Marx's vision of communism. Marx immediately goes on to say that it is out of this very contradiction between the interest of the individual and the community that the state develops as an independent entity. So an understanding of how this contradiction can be overcome should enable us to understand the famous Marxist doctrine that under communism the state will be superseded.

In proposing a solution to the problem of the individual and the community, Marx was contributing to a tradition in moral philosophy going back at least to Plato. Plato had argued that personal happiness is to be found in virtuous conduct and in serving one's community. He thus found harmony between the individual's interest in happiness and the needs of the community. But Plato's arguments did not convince later philosophers.

Marx thought the division between individual interest and community interest was a feature of a particular stage of human development, rather than an inevitable aspect of social existence, a feature which had existed ever since the break-up of very simple societies which had lived communally, without private ownership and division of labour. Capitalism, however, heightened the conflict by turning everything into a commodity, leaving 'no other nexus between man and man than naked self-interest, than callous "cash payment"' (*CM* 223).

How did Marx think the opposition between private and communal interests could be overcome? Obviously the abolition of private property could play a part – it is not so easy to feather one's own nest if there is nothing one can call one's own to feather it with. But the change would have to go deeper, for even without private property people could pursue their own interests by trying to get as much as they could for themselves (for immediate consumption if the abolition of private property made hoarding impossible) or by shirking their share of the work necessary to keep the community going. To alter this, nothing short of a radical transformation of human nature would suffice.

Here the materialist conception of history underpins the possibility of communism. According to Marx's view of history, as the economic basis of society alters, so all consciousness alters. Greed, egoism, and envy are not ingrained forever in the character of human beings. They would disappear in a society in which private property and private means of production were replaced with communal property and socially organized means of production. We would lose our preoccupation with our private interests. Citizens of the new society would find their own happiness in working for the good of all. Hence a communist society would have a new ethical basis. It has been claimed – by Lenin among others – that Marxism is a scientific system, free from any ethical judgements or postulates. This is obviously nonsense. Marx did not just predict that capitalism would be overthrown and replaced by communism. He judged the change to be desirable. He did not need to make this judgement explicit, as it was implied by everything he wrote about capitalism and communism, and by his unceasing political activity. Marx's ethical attitudes are woven into his conception of human progress through alienation to the final state of complete freedom.

The belief that Marxism contains no ethical judgements derives from some comments made by Marx and Engels. In *The Communist Manifesto*, for instance, morality is listed together with law and religion as 'bourgeois prejudices, behind which lurk in ambush just as many bourgeois interests' (*CM* 230). It is true that for Marx morality is part of the ideological superstructure of society, is determined by the economic basis, and serves to promote the interests of the ruling class. But it does not follow from this that all morality is to be rejected. What has to be rejected is morality that serves the interests of the ruling class. This includes all dominant moralities up to now. Once communism has been established and classes have disappeared, however, we can pass beyond class morality, to what Engels called 'a really human morality'.

As with communism in general, so with communist morality one can only guess at its detailed content. Communism would differ from all previous societies in that there would be no false consciousness. False consciousness involves failing to see things as they really are. It comes about because a society's superstructure can conceal the real basis of the society – as the legal freedom of the worker to sell his labour to whomever he likes on whatever terms he likes conceals the fact that he is really no more able to avoid exploitation by capitalists than the feudal serf is free to avoid working on the land of his lord. Class morality adds an extra layer of false consciousness, leading the worker to believe that, for example, the capitalist has a moral right to the proceeds of his investment.

With communist production there would be no exploitation to be concealed. Everything would really be as it appeared to be. Moral illusions would crumble along with the religious illusions against which the Young Hegelians argued so fiercely. The new human morality would not hypocritically cloak sectional interests in a universal guise. It would genuinely serve the interests of all human beings. Its universal form would be matched by a universal content.

The new morality would have a character quite different from previous moralities, different even from moralities like utilitarianism which proclaim their equal concern for all. Though Marx was as scornful of utilitarianism as of any other ethical theory, his scorn was directed at the utilitarian conception of the general interest rather than at the basic utilitarian idea of maximizing happiness – in fact Marx refers to this idea as 'a homespun commonplace', which does not imply that he disagrees with it (C I 609). But in capitalist society, to propose that people act for the general interest is often to propose that they work against their own interest, as they conceive it. Under such conditions the very idea of morality implies something burdensome and contrary to our own interests. Under communism this aspect of morality will vanish as the gulf between individual interest and universal interest vanishes. Morality will cease to be a dictate from without, and become an expression of our chief wants as social beings.

It has been said that later in life Marx developed a less Utopian view of communism, but it is difficult to find much evidence of this. There is one passage in the third volume of *Capital* which, in contrast to the claim of the *Economic and Philosophic Manuscripts*, sees the conflict between freedom and necessity as ineliminable. This is the passage, already cited, in which Marx says that freedom begins 'only where labour which is determined by necessity and mundane considerations ceases'. He goes on to say that it is part of 'the very nature of things' that when we are producing to satisfy our needs we are not free. Shortening the working day is, therefore, the prerequisite of freedom (C III 496–7). This implies that the conflict between freedom and necessity cannot be overcome, and the best that can be done is to reduce the amount of necessary labour to a minimum, thereby increasing the time that we are free. It is a statement which contrasts oddly with what Marx says about communism in his comments on the Gotha Program – also a late work – which are as optimistic as any of the early statements. There Marx foresees the end of the 'enslaving subordination of the individual to the division of labour' and a time when labour will become 'not only a means of life, but life's prime want' (GP 569). The idea of labour as 'life's prime want' is very different from the clock-watching attitude that takes the shortening of the working day as the prerequisite of freedom.

It is, incidentally, in these comments on the Gotha Program that Marx proposes the celebrated principle of distribution for a communist society: 'from each according to his ability, to each according to his needs'. The principle is not original to Marx, and Marx places little emphasis upon it. He refers to it only in order to criticize those socialists who worry too much about how goods would be distributed in a socialist society. Marx thought it a mistake to bother about working out a fair or just principle of distribution. He was even prepared to allow that, given the capitalist mode of production, capitalist distribution was the only one that was 'fair'. His point was that production was what mattered, and once 'the productive forces have increased with the all-round development of the individual, and all the springs of co-operative wealth flow more abundantly', distribution will look after itself (GP 566).

Everything Marx says about communism is premised on material abundance. Remember that it is the development of the forces of production that, according to the materialist theory of history, is the driving force behind historical change. The change from one form of society to another occurs when the existing structure of society acts as a fetter on the further development of the productive forces. But communism is the final form of society. Building on the dramatic advances so ruthlessly made by capitalism, communism allows the forces of production to develop to their fullest possible extent. Production will be co-operatively planned for the benefit of all, not wasted in socially fruitless competition between individual capitalists for their own private ends. There will be no crises of overproduction, as there are in unplanned economies. The reserve army of unemployed workers required by capitalism to keep labour cheap and available will become productive. Mechanization and automation will continue to develop as they had developed under capitalism, though without their degrading effect on the workers (unfortunately Marx does not tell us how these effects would be avoided, but presumably it would be by a drastic reduction in the hours of necessary labour). No longer will surplus-value be extracted from the workers to line the pockets of the capitalists. The working class will receive the full use-value of its labour, subject only to a deduction for future social investment. We will control our economy, instead of being controlled by it.

Material abundance and the transformation of human nature provide the basis for Marx's claim that the state as we know it would cease to exist under communism. This would not happen immediately, for at first the proletariat would have to assert itself over the other classes, in order to abolish capitalist forms of production. This would be the 'dictatorship of the proletariat'. But once capitalist production had been replaced by socialist production the division of society into classes would disappear, along with conflicts between individual and social interests. There would be no need for political power in the Marxist sense of the organized power of one class used to oppress another. Nor, given Marx's idea that communism would come first to the most industrially advanced societies, and would be international in character, would there be any need for the state in the sense of an organization existing to defend the nation against attacks from other nations. Relieved from oppressive conditions that bring their interests into conflict, people would voluntarily co-operate with each other. The political state resting on armed force would become obsolete; its place would be taken by 'an association, in which the free development of each is the condition for the free development of all' (CM 238).

Chapter 10
An Assessment

Any exposition of Marx's ideas is also an assessment of them. In arguing that Marx's main achievements – his theory of history and his economics – are not scientific discoveries, I have already rejected the accolade bestowed on Marx by Engels, confirmed by Lenin, and echoed by orthodox Marxist-Leninists ever since. But if Marx did not make scientific discoveries about economics and society, what did he achieve? Is his system now only a historical curiosity? In this concluding section I shall state my view of which elements of Marx's thought remain valuable, and which need to be revised or scrapped.

First, though, it is necessary to say a little more about Marx as a scientist; for it cannot be denied that Marx thought of his own theories as 'scientific', and based predictions about the future of capitalism on them. He predicted that:

The income gap between capitalists and workers will increase.

More and more independent producers will be forced down into the proletariat, leaving a few rich capitalists and a mass of poor workers.

Workers' wages will, with short-lived exceptions, remain at subsistence level.

13. Marx's grave at Highgate Cemetery in London

The rate of profit will fall.

Capitalism will collapse because of its internal contradictions.

Proletarian revolutions will occur in the most industrially advanced countries.

More than a century after Marx made these predictions, most of them are so plainly mistaken that one can only wonder why anyone sympathetic to Marx would attempt to argue that his greatness lies in the scientific aspects of his work. Judged by the standards of Marx's time, the gap between rich and poor has narrowed dramatically throughout the industrialized world. Though the gap has widened again in the last decade of the twentieth century, it is still nothing like what it was during the nineteenth century. This is largely because real wages have risen. Factory workers today earn considerably more than they need in order to remain alive and reproducing. The rate of profit has not gone into a steady decline. Capitalism has gone through several crises, but nowhere has it collapsed as a result of its alleged internal contradictions. Proletarian revolutions have broken out in the less developed nations, rather than the more developed ones.

Nevertheless, the fate of Marx's predictions is not a ground for disregarding his ideas as a whole, any more than the fact that Jesus thought the second coming would take place in the lifetime of those he addressed is a reason for taking no further heed of Christianity. Such errors merely show that those who made them are fallible. It is better to think of Marx as a philosopher – in the broadest sense – rather than as a scientist. We have seen how Marx's predictions were derived from his application of Hegel's philosophy to the progress of human history and the economics of capitalism. No one now thinks of Hegel as a scientist, although Hegel, like Marx, described his work as 'scientific'. The German term they both used includes any serious, systematic study, and in that sense, of course, Marx and Hegel were both scientists; but we now regard Hegel as a philosopher, and we should think of Marx primarily in the same way.

As a philosopher, Marx's work endures. It has altered our understanding of our own nature, and deepened our grasp of what it is to be free.

Let us take the second of these first, for freedom was Marx's central concern (paradoxical as this may seem when we look at the regimes that profess to follow his ideas). The significance of Marx's idea of freedom is best appreciated by contrasting it with the standard liberal notion of freedom accepted – in Marx's time and in our own – by those who oppose government interference with the free market. According to this view, I am free so long as I am not subject to deliberate interference from other people. Of course, there have to be limits to this freedom. The government may properly interfere with me if, for instance, I assault my neighbours; then I am deliberately interfering with others and my own freedom can be restricted to ensure greater freedom for all. This is consistent with holding that freedom is at its maximum when each individual is able to act without deliberate interference from others.

This liberal conception of freedom fits perfectly with the economic theories of defenders of unrestrained capitalism, for they portray capitalism as the outcome of the free choices of millions of individuals. The capitalist merely offers people work at, say, £1 an hour, for forty hours a week. Anyone can choose, without interference from others, to accept or reject this offer. If some accept it, the capitalist uses their labour for his own purposes, say, to make shirts. He offers these shirts for sale at a certain price, and again anyone can freely choose whether or not to buy them at this price. And anyone who thinks he can do better than the capitalists now in business is free to set up his own enterprise.

This is not how capitalism really works, of course, but it shows how the liberal view of freedom can be used to provide a defence of capitalism which is immune to objections along the line that capitalists are greedy people who exploit the poor by selling at exorbitant prices. Defenders of capitalism can readily admit that some capitalists may be greedy, but they can also point out that no one is forced to work for or buy from any individual capitalist. So the greed of individual capitalists is not a reason for condemning the free enterprise system.

Marx saw that within its own terms this defence of capitalism is coherent; but he also saw that from a broader, historical perspective, the liberal definition of freedom is open to a fundamental objection. To explain his objection, I shall switch to a more homely example. Suppose I live in the suburbs and work in the city. I could drive my car to work, or take the bus. I prefer not to wait around for the bus, and so I take my car. Fifty thousand other people living in my suburb face the same choice and make the same decision. The road to town is choked with cars. It takes each of us an hour to travel ten miles.

In this situation, according to the liberal conception of freedom, we have all chosen freely. No one deliberately interfered with our choices. Yet the outcome is something none of us want. If we all went by bus, the roads would be empty and we could cover the distance in twenty minutes. Even with the inconvenience of waiting at the bus stop, we would all prefer that. We are, of course, free to alter our choice of transportation, but what can we do? While so many cars slow the bus down, why should any individual choose differently? The liberal conception of freedom has led to a paradox: we have each chosen in our own interests, but the result is in no one's interest. Individual rationality, collective irrationality.

The solution, obviously, is for us all to get together and make a collective decision. As individuals we are unable to bring about the situation we desire. Together we can achieve what we want, subject only to the physical limits of our resources and technology. In this example, we can all agree to use the bus.

Marx saw that capitalism involves this kind of collective irrationality. In pre-capitalist systems it was obvious that most people did not control their own destiny – under feudalism, for instance, serfs had to work for their lords. Capitalism seems different because people are in theory free to work for themselves or for others as they choose. Yet most workers have as little control over their lives as feudal serfs. This is not because they have chosen badly. Nor is it because of the physical limits of our resources and technology. It is because the cumulative effect of countless individual choices is a society that no one – not even the capitalists – has chosen. Where those who hold the liberal conception of freedom would say we are free because we are not subject to deliberate interference by other humans, Marx says we are not free because we do not control our own society. Economic relations between human beings determine not only our wages and our prospects of finding work, but also our politics, our religion, and our ideas. These economic relations force us into a situation in which we compete with each other instead of co-operating for the good of all. These conditions nullify technical advances in the use of our resources. Rationally organized, industrialization should enable us to enjoy an abundance of material goods with a minimum of effort; under capitalism, however, these advances simply reduce the value of the commodity produced, which means that the worker must work just as long for the same wage. (In saying this, Marx was supposing that real wages would remain around subsistence level; in fact the increase in productivity has allowed real wages to rise.) Worse still, the absence of any overall planning or direction in the economy leads to crises of overproduction – that overproduction can cause a crisis is in itself a clear indication of an irrational system – and to recessions in which the economy operates in a manner that neither workers nor capitalists desire. (Here Marx's point retains some truth, as governments still have difficulty in eliminating unemployment while restraining inflation.)

Economic relations appear to us blind natural forces. We do not see them as restricting our freedom – and indeed on the liberal conception of freedom they do not restrict our freedom, since they are not the result of deliberate human interference. Marx himself is quite explicit that the capitalist is not individually responsible for the economic relations of his society, but is controlled by these relations as much as the workers are (*C* I 10). Yet these economic relations are our own unwitting creations, not deliberately chosen but nevertheless the outcome of our own individual choices and thus potentially subject to our will. We are not truly free until, instead of letting our creations control us, we collectively take control of them. Hence the significance of a planned economy. In an unplanned economy human beings unwittingly grant the market control over their lives; planning the economy is a reassertion of human sovereignty and an essential step towards true human freedom.

Marx's penetrating insight into the nature of freedom remains a challenge to any liberal political philosophy. It is the core of Marx's attack on alienation in the 1844 *Manuscripts*, as it is the core of his critique of the free market in *Capital*. If Marx has any claim to a place alongside Hobbes, Locke, Rousseau, and Hegel as a major figure in Western political thought, it must rest on his attack on the liberal conception of freedom. All the same, the alternative conception of freedom Marx espoused contains within it a difficulty Marx never sufficiently appreciated, a difficulty which can be linked with the tragic mutation of Marx's views into a prop for murderously authoritarian regimes. This is the problem of obtaining the co-operation of each individual in the joint endeavour of controlling our society.

Return for a moment to our example of the commuters. They hold a meeting. All agree that it would be better to leave their cars at home. They part, rejoicing at the prospect of no more traffic jams. But in the privacy of their own homes, some reason to themselves as follows: 'If everyone else is going to take the bus tomorrow, the roads will be empty. So I'll take my car. Then I'll have the convenience of door-to-door transportation *and* the advantage of a traffic-free run which will get me to work in less time than if I took the bus.' From a self-interested point of view this reasoning is correct. As long as most take the bus, a few others can obtain the benefits of the socially minded behaviour of the majority, without giving up anything themselves.

What should the majority do about this? Should they leave it up to the individual conscience to decide whether to abuse the system in this manner? If they do, there is a risk that the system will break down – once a few take their own cars, others will soon follow, for no one likes to be taken advantage of. Or should the majority attempt to coerce the minority into taking the bus? That is the easy way out. It can be done in the name of freedom for all; but it may lead to freedom for none.

Marx was devoted to the cause of human freedom. When asked, in a Victorian parlour game, to name the vice he most detested, he replied: 'Servility'; and as his favourite motto he put down: 'De omnibus dubitandum' – 'You must have doubts about everything' (ME 456–7). Though his own personality had an authoritarian streak, there can be little doubt he would have been appalled at the authority Lenin and Stalin wielded in his name. (Marx would probably have been an early victim of the purges.) Marx thought that under communism the state would cease to exist as a political entity. Coercion would be unnecessary because communism would end the conflict between individual interests and the common good. The end of this conflict would bring with it the end of any threat of a conflict between the freedom of the community to control its own economic and social life, and the freedom of the individual to do as he or she pleases.

Here – Marx's second lasting contribution to modern thought – his view of human nature – ties in with his idea of freedom. Marx's theory that human nature is not for ever fixed, but alters in accordance with the economic and social conditions of each period, holds out the prospect of transforming society by changing the economic basis of such human traits as greed, egoism, and ambition. Marx expected the abolition of private property and the institution of common ownership of the means of production and exchange to bring about a society in which people were motivated more by a desire for the good of all than by a specific desire for their own individual good. In this way individual and common interests could be harmonized.

Marx's view of human nature is now so widely accepted that a return to a pre-Marxist conception of human nature is unthinkable. Though Marx's own theory is not scientific, it laid the foundations for a new social science which would explore the relations between such apparently unconnected areas of life as the tools people use to produce food and their political and religious beliefs. Undoubtedly this is a fruitful area for historians and social scientists to investigate. In opening it up, Marx shattered the assumption that our intellectual and spiritual lives are entirely independent of our economic existence. If 'Know thyself' is the first imperative of philosophy, Marx's contribution to our self-understanding is another reason for ranking him highly among philosophers.

Once Marx has been given due credit for making us aware of the economic and social forces that may influence us, however, it has to be added that his own view of human nature is false. Human nature is not as pliable as he believed. Egoism, for instance, is not eliminated by economic reorganization or by material abundance. When basic needs are satisfied, new 'needs' emerge. In our society, people want not simply clothes, but fashionable clothes; not shelter, but a house to display their wealth and taste. It is not just advertising that leads to these desires, for they emerge in the non-capitalist world as well, often in the face of disapproval from the official ideology. Unless rigid uniformity is imposed – and perhaps even then – these desires will find an outlet. And it will never be possible to satisfy everyone's material desires. How could we provide everyone with a house in a secluded position overlooking the sea, but within easy reach of the city?

In different societies, egoistic desires will take different forms. This does not show that they can be abolished altogether, but only that they are the expression of a more basic desire. There is, for instance, more than simple greed behind our insatiable urge for consumer goods. There is also the desire for status, and perhaps sometimes a desire for the power which status can bring. No doubt capitalism accentuates these desires. There are societies in which competition for status and power are much more restrained. There may even be societies lacking any such competition. Yet desires for status and power exist in many human beings, in a range of different societies. They tend to surface despite repeated efforts to suppress them. No society, no matter how egalitarian its rhetoric, has succeeded in abolishing the distinction between ruler and ruled. Nor has any society succeeded in making this distinction *merely* a matter of who leads and who follows: to be a ruler gives one special status and, usually, special privileges. During the Communist era, important officials in the Soviet Union had access to special shops selling delicacies unavailable to ordinary citizens; before China allowed capitalist enterprises in its economy, travelling by car was a luxury limited to tourists and those high in the party hierarchy (and their families). Throughout the 'communist' nations, the abolition of the old ruling class was followed by the rise of a new class of party bosses and well-placed bureaucrats, whose behaviour and life-style came more and more to resemble that of their much-denounced predecessors. In the end, nobody believed in the system any more. That, coupled with its inability to match the productivity of the less bureaucratically controlled, more egoistically driven capitalist economies, led to its downfall.

I point to these failings of the allegedly communist world not in order to say that this was the kind of society Marx wanted – obviously, it wasn't – but to ask what there is to be learnt from these historical experiments. Before answering this question, however, we should note that the prevalence of hierarchy is not limited to human societies. There are clear hierarchies among most social birds and mammals,

14. Joseph Stalin (1879–1953), the Soviet dictator, at work in his office, with Marx's portrait above his head

including those species most nearly related to human beings. Farmers have always known that barnyard flocks of hens develop a 'pecking order' in which each hen has a rank, allowing her to peck at and drive away from food birds below her in rank, but to be pecked by, and forced to give up food to, those above her. More careful studies have shown that similar hierarchies exist among wolves, deer, lions, baboons, and chimpanzees, to name only a few of the species studied.

So we have evidence that was not available to Marx – evidence of the failure of deliberate attempts to create egalitarian societies on the basis of the abolition of private ownership of the means of production and exchange; and evidence of the hierarchical nature of non-human societies. The evidence is not yet all in; but we have enough to reach the provisional judgement that it will not be as easy as Marx thought to bring the conflicting interests of human beings into harmony.

If this is right, it has far-reaching consequences for Marx's positive proposals. If changing the economic basis of society will not bring the individual to see that his own interests and the interests of society are the same, communism as Marx conceived it must be abandoned. Except perhaps for the brief period in which the economic structure of the society was in the process of transformation to social ownership, Marx never intended a communist society to force the individual to work against his or her own interests for the collective good. The need to use coercion would signify not the overcoming of alienation, but the continuing alienation of man from man; a coercive society would not be the riddle of history resolved, but merely the riddle restated in a new form; it would not end class rule, but would substitute a new ruling class for the old one. While it is absurd to blame Marx for something he did not foresee and certainly would have condemned if he had foreseen it, the distance between Marx's predicted communist society and the form taken by 'communism' in the twentieth century may in the end be traceable to Marx's misconception of the flexibility of human nature.

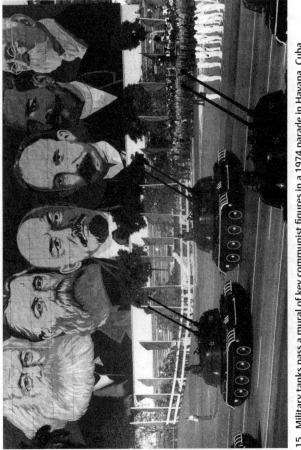

15. Military tanks pass a mural of key communist figures in a 1974 parade in Havana, Cuba, marking the anniversary of the Revolution

It is both sad and ironic to read today some marginal jottings Marx made in 1874, while reading Bakunin's *Statism and Anarchy*. Marx copied out passages from this work by his anarchist rival from the days of the first International, and then made his own comments on each passage. Thus the jottings read like a dialogue, one section of which goes like this:

> *Bakunin:* Universal suffrage by the whole people of representatives and rulers of the state – this is the last word of the Marxists as well as of the democratic school. They are lies behind which lurks the despotism of a governing minority, lies all the more dangerous in that this minority appears as the expression of the so-called people's will.
>
> *Marx:* Under collective property, the so-called will of the people disappears in order to make way for the real will of the co-operative.
>
> *Bakunin:* Result: rule of the great majority of the people by a privileged minority. But, the Marxists say, this minority will consist of workers. Yes, indeed, but of ex-workers who, once they become only representatives or rulers of the people, cease to be workers.
>
> *Marx:* No more than a manufacturer today ceases to be a capitalist when he becomes a member of the municipal council.
>
> *Bakunin:* And from the heights of the state they begin to look down upon the whole common world of the workers. From that time on they represent not the people but themselves and their own claims to govern the people. Those who can doubt this know nothing at all about human nature.
>
> *Marx:* If Mr Bakunin were familiar just with the position of a manager in a workers' co-operative, he could send all his nightmares about authority to the devil. He should have asked himself: what form can administrative functions take, on the basis of this workers' state – if he wants to call it that?
>
> (B 563)

The tragedy of Marxism is that a century after Marx wrote these words, our experience of the rule of workers in several different countries bears out Bakunin's objections, rather than Marx's replies. Marx saw that capitalism is a wasteful, irrational system, a system which controls us when we should be controlling it. That insight is still valid; but we can now see that the construction of a free and equal society is a more difficult task than Marx realized.

Note on Sources

The quotations from Engels on pp. 16 and 23 are from 'Ludwig Feuerbach and the End of Classical German Philosophy', in K. Marx, F. Engels, *Selected Works* (Foreign Languages Publishing House, Moscow, 1951), Vol. 2, pp. 365–8. The description of Moses Hess as the first to reach communism by 'the philosophic path' (see p. 27) comes from 'Progress of Social Reform on the Continent', an article Engels wrote for *The New Moral World*, a small English journal, in 1843; it is quoted in Robert Tucker's *Philosophy and Myth in Karl Marx* (Cambridge University Press, Cambridge, 1961), p. 107. Engels refers to Marx denying that he is a Marxist (see p. 51) in a letter to Starkenburg, 25 January 1894; Engels' letters to Schmidt (5 August 1890), to Bloch (21 September 1890) and to Mehring (14 April 1893) also deal with the interpretation of historical materialism. All are reprinted in L. S. Feuer (ed.), *Marx & Engels: Basic Writings on Politics and Philosophy* (Doubleday Anchor, New York, 1959). The expression 'a really human morality' cited on p. 82 comes from Engels's *Anti-Dühring*, also reprinted in Feuer, at p. 272.

The quotation from Hegel on p. 20 is from *The Philosophy of History* (trans. J. Sibree, ed. C. J. Friedrich, Dover, New York, 1956), p. 19.

The contemporary economist quoted on p. 76 is Paul Samuelson, writing in the *American Economic Review*, vol. 47 (1957), p. 911.

Further Reading

Writings by Marx

Marx wrote so much that the definitive edition of all the writings of Marx and Engels, now in the process of publication in East Germany, will take twenty-five years and a hundred volumes to complete. A more modest English edition of *Collected Works* began appearing in 1975, published by Lawrence and Wishart; it will eventually contain about fifty volumes. Meanwhile the English reader must make do with complete editions of the major works, and selections from others. As the list of abbreviations on pp. ix–x suggests, I regard *Karl Marx: Selected Writings* edited by David McLellan (Oxford University Press, Oxford, 1977) as the best single-volume collection. Lewis Feuer's *Marx & Engels: Basic Writings on Politics and Philosophy* (Doubleday Anchor, New York, 1959) has a good selection of the 'classic' writings of the mature Marx but for a comprehensive picture it needs to be supplemented by a collection of Marx's earlier writings, like Loyd Easton and Kurt Guddat (eds), *Writings of the Young Marx on Philosophy and Society* (Doubleday Anchor, New York, 1967).

There are many editions of Marx's most famous works. The *Communist Manifesto* is a good place to begin reading Marx. It is available in a Penguin edition, edited by A. J. P. Taylor (Harmondsworth, 1967), and is reprinted in its entirety in McLellan's and many other volumes of selected writings. Having read the *Manifesto* and some selections from other texts, the reader may like to try the first volume of *Capital*. It is not as difficult as one might imagine, and is again available in a number of different editions, of which the Moore and Aveling translation published in Moscow is the most commonly used.

For those who want something in between one and fifty volumes, the Marx Library, published by Penguin in Britain and Vintage in the USA, is an eight-volume collection that includes the complete *Grundrisse* and a good selection of Marx's journalism and political writings.

Writings about Marx

If the writings by Marx and Engels take up a hundred volumes, those about Marx must run into the tens of thousands. Below is a *very* brief selection of some better recent books. Although older works are interesting because they enable us to see how earlier generations conceived Marx, their ignorance of his unpublished early writings and of the *Grundrisse* make them an unreliable guide to the basis of Marx's views.

For books on Marx's life, there is little need to go beyond David McLellan's outstanding *Karl Marx: His Life and Thought* (Macmillan, London, 1973). A slightly less sympathetic alternative is Saul K. Padover, *The Man Marx* (McGraw-Hill, New York, 1978). Jerrold Seigel's *Marx's Fate* (Princeton University Press, Princeton, 1978) may appeal to those who favour psychoanalytic biographies. Among older works, Isaiah Berlin's *Karl Marx: His Life and Environment* (first edition 1939, fourth edition, Oxford University Press, Oxford, 1978) has lost none of its flowing style in several updatings.

On Marx's thought, as distinct from his life, Robert Tucker, in *Philosophy and Myth in Karl Marx* (Cambridge University Press, Cambridge, 1961), was among the first to emphasize the continuity of Marx's ideas, from his earliest Hegelian essays to *Capital*. Tucker's interpretation is novel, if at times too dramatic. David McLellan's *The Young Hegelians and Karl*

Marx (Macmillan, London, 1969) gives useful background to Marx's intellectual development. Bertell Ollman, *Alienation: Marx's Conception of Man in Capitalist Society* (second edition, Cambridge University Press, Cambridge, 1977), is more readable than most works on alienation.

To balance the Hegelian emphasis of these works, G. A. Cohen's *Karl Marx's Theory of History: A Defence* (Oxford University Press, Oxford, 1979) argues brilliantly for a more old-fashioned interpretation of Marxism as a scientific theory of history, an interpretation often known – disparagingly – as 'technological determinism'. Melvin Rader's *Marx's Interpretation of History* (Oxford University Press, New York, 1979) presents a wider range of possible interpretations.

Finally, those interested in the entire sweep of Marxist theory, from the founders through its 'Golden Age' to its dissolution into Soviet ideology, should not miss *Main Currents of Marxism* by Lemek Kolakowski (3 vols, Oxford University Press, Oxford, 1978).

Index

A

'alienation' 18–36, 39, 46–7, 60,
        68, 76, 92, 97

B

Bakunin, M. A. 99–100
Bauer, Bruno 21–3, 25–8, 39, 43
Berlin 3, 8, 16, 21
Brussels 7–9

C

Capital 7, 10–12, 32, 38, 51, 55,
        59–60, 64, 67–76, 83, 92
capitalism, capitalists 10, 33,
        36–8, 41, 48–50, 59–78,
        80–93, 95–7, 100
Civil War in France, The 11
communism, communists 1, 6–8,
        15, 27, 37–8, 43, 78–85, 92,
        94–6
Communist League 8–9
Communist Manifesto, The 8, 50,
        82, 85
conservatism, conservatives 1
*Contribution to the Critique of
        Political Economy, A* 10, 44,
        47–8, 67
Critique of the Gotha Program 15,
        84

D

Darwin, Charles 38, 47, 53
Democritus 5

Demuth, Frederick (illegitimate
        son) 9
Demuth, Helene 9
dialectical materialism 17, 40–1

E

*Economic and Philosophic
        Manuscripts of 1844* 32–8,
        43, 55, 60, 64, 79, 83, 92
economics, economists 3–7, 10,
        27, 30–8, 48–56, 59–77,
        81–2, 86–8, 91–2
*Eighteenth Brumaire of Louis
        Bonaparte, The* 50
Engels, R. 6–12, 16, 23, 27, 38–44,
        47, 51–5, 74, 82, 85
    oration at Marx's funeral 52,
        66, 78
England 7–8, 56–7, 73
Epicurus 3

F

feudalism 49, 71–2
Feuerbach, L. A. 23–8, 32–5, 41–3
Fichte, J. G. 41
First International, the, *see*
        International Workingmen's
        Association
France 8, 10–11, 29, 31

G

Germany 5–6, 9, 16–17, 28–31
German Ideology, The 7–8, 41,
        44–6, 52, 55, 60, 64, 80
'Gotha Program', the 12
Grundrisse 51, 53, 64–6, 70

H

Hegel, G. W. F. 5, 16–27, 28–32,
    34–5, 37, 40–3, 54–6, 64, 70,
    88–9, 92
Hess, Moses 27
Hitler, A. 1
Hobbes, T. 92
Holy Family, The 7, 39–41, 44, 60

I

International Workingmen's
    Association (the First
    International) 11, 99

J

Jews, Jewishness, Judaism 3,
    25–7, 41

K

Kautsky, K. 59

L

Lenin, V. L. 81, 86, 93
Locke, J. 92
London 9–11

M

Manchester 6–7
Marx, Edgar (son) 9
Marx, Eleanor (daughter) 10
Marx, Jenny (daughter) 9, 10,
    12–15
Marx, Jenny (wife) *see*
    Westphalen, Jenny von
Marx, Karl
  birth and parentage 3

and communism 1, 6–8, 15,
    37–8, 43, 79–85, 92, 94–6
death of wife and daughter 15
and economics 6–7, 10, 27,
    30–8, 48–56, 59–77, 86, 91
finances 3–7, 9, 10–12
and freedom 25, 37, 47, 56,
    72, 82–3, 89–93
influence of 1–3, 86–100
influence of Feuerbach 23–4,
    34–5
influence of Hegel 16–18, 24,
    35, 64
journalism 4–6, 8–9, 60
marriage 3
the materialist conception of
    history 38–59, 78, 81, 84, 86
and philosophy 6, 16, 28–31,
    88–9, 92, 94
and the proletariat 28–36,
    39–43, 50, 57, 85
relationship with Engels 6–9,
    11, 51
university studies 3–5, 16, 21
writings 6–8, 12–15, 38, 29–43,
    67
Marx, Laura (daughter) 7, 10, 15
Marxism, Marxists 1, 28, 32, 37,
    43, 51, 61, 74, 80, 85–6, 94,
    99
materialist conception of history,
    see Marx, Karl
Mussolini, B. 1

N

nationalism 1

O

'On the Jewish Question' 25,
29, 41

P

Paris 6–8, 31–2
    Commune 11
philosophy, philosophers 2–6,
    16–31, 40–3, 54–5, 57, 64,
    80, 89, 94
    of history 37, 43
Plato 80
Poverty of Philosophy, The 60
proletariat, the 28–36, 40–2, 50,
    57, 78, 85–8
Proudhon, P. J. 8, 36, 39

R

religion 3, 21–8, 34, 42–4, 49,
    52–3
revolution, revolutionaries 1, 6,
    9–10, 12, 31, 43, 74, 78–9
    French 1848 8
    industrial 73, 75
Ricardo, David 62–4, 68, 75
Rousseau, J.-J. 92
Ruge, Arnold 25

S

Say, J.-B. 33
Smith, Adam 33, 68
socialism, socialists 6, 12–15, 25,
    43, 79, 84
Stalin, I. V. 93

T

'Theses on Feuerbach' 41–3
'Towards a Critique of Hegel's
    Philosophy of Right:
    Introduction' 28, 31, 43

U

utilitarianism 83

V

Vogt, Karl 10

W

Wage Labour and Capital 60–4
'Wages, Price and Profit' 64
Westphalen, Jenny von (wife)
    3–9, 15

Y

Young Hegelians 20–2, 25, 27, 82

Marx

Expand your collection of
VERY SHORT INTRODUCTIONS

1. Classics
2. Music
3. Buddhism
4. Literary Theory
5. Hinduism
6. Psychology
7. Islam
8. Politics
9. Theology
10. Archaeology
11. Judaism
12. Sociology
13. The Koran
14. The Bible
15. Social and Cultural Anthropology
16. History
17. Roman Britain
18. The Anglo-Saxon Age
19. Medieval Britain
20. The Tudors
21. Stuart Britain
22. Eighteenth-Century Britain
23. Nineteenth-Century Britain
24. Twentieth-Century Britain
25. Heidegger
26. Ancient Philosophy
27. Socrates
28. Marx
29. Logic
30. Descartes
31. Machiavelli
32. Aristotle
33. Hume
34. Nietzsche
35. Darwin
36. The European Union
37. Gandhi
38. Augustine
39. Intelligence
40. Jung
41. Buddha
42. Paul
43. Continental Philosophy
44. Galileo
45. Freud
46. Wittgenstein
47. Indian Philosophy
48. Rousseau
49. Hegel
50. Kant
51. Cosmology
52. Drugs
53. Russian Literature
54. The French Revolution
55. Philosophy
56. Barthes
57. Animal Rights
58. Kierkegaard
59. Russell
60. Shakespeare
61. Clausewitz
62. Schopenhauer
63. The Russian Revolution
64. Hobbes
65. World Music
66. Mathematics
67. Philosophy of Science
68. Cryptography
69. Quantum Theory
70. Spinoza

71. Choice Theory
72. Architecture
73. Poststructuralism
74. Postmodernism
75. Democracy
76. Empire
77. Fascism
78. Terrorism
79. Plato
80. Ethics
81. Emotion
82. Northern Ireland
83. Art Theory
84. Locke
85. Modern Ireland
86. Globalization
87. Cold War
88. The History of Astronomy
89. Schizophrenia
90. The Earth
91. Engels
92. British Politics
93. Linguistics
94. The Celts
95. Ideology
96. Prehistory
97. Political Philosophy
98. Postcolonialism
99. Atheism
100. Evolution
101. Molecules
102. Art History
103. Presocratic Philosophy
104. The Elements
105. Dada and Surrealism
106. Egyptian Myth
107. Christian Art

Visit the
VERY SHORT
INTRODUCTIONS
Web site

www.oup.co.uk/vsi

➤ **Information** about all published titles

➤ News of **forthcoming books**

➤ **Extracts** from the books, including titles not yet published

➤ **Reviews** and views

➤ **Links** to other **web sites** and main OUP web page

➤ Information about **VSIs in translation**

➤ **Contact** the editors

➤ **Order** other **VSIs** on-line